# Perfectly Pareve

## COOKBOOK

# Eileen Goltz

# Perfectly Pareve

## COOKBOOK

**Illustrated by Tamar Silverstein**

FELDHEIM PUBLISHERS
JERUSALEM    NEW YORK

ISBN 1-58330-447-9
First published 2001
Copyright © 2001 by Eileen Goltz

FELDHEIM PUBLISHERS
POB 35002 / Jerusalem, Israel
202 Airport Executive Park, Nanuet, NY 10954

www.feldheim.com

*Printed in Israel*

# Contents

# Acknowledgments

No one can succeed alone. I've been blessed with a great deal of love and support from my family and friends. They've listened to me moan and groan and have tasted tons of disasters. So to:

Mom and Dad, always there, always supportive,

Larry, Shlomo and Avi, my life, my family and still my biggest fans,

Lois, Hal and Robbie, you keep me grounded and keep me going,

Fred and Mindy, friends forever and the ones who started it all,

Josh and Donna, always ready with an ear, a shoulder and a great joke,

Rick and Marsha, special friends, editors and our home away from home,

Connie and Alan for a daily dose of common sense and support,

Laurel and Jim, wonderful friends, neighbors and taste-testers extraordinaire,

Alan and Janice, always honest, always there, always amazing,

Arlene and Jere, 12's forever and may we always root for the clock,

Virginia — just the best,

Uncle Burt and Aunt Babs, so much more than just family,

From the bottom of my heart, I thank you all!

## Introduction

The Jewish dietary laws prohibit eating milk and meat — and any dairy and meat dishes — together. Those foods that are neither dairy nor meat are called pareve (a Yiddish word).

*Perfectly Pareve* began as a quest for a few good pareve recipes that I could serve at a wedding I was catering. Cooking school had taught me the basics and thirteen years in the catering business had given me the experience, but quite frankly, the pareve recipes I had been using weren't very exciting or special. One bride wanted her wedding to be *très* gourmet and I was determined to rise to the challenge. I spent three weeks searching for ingredients, creating and altering recipes and then testing recipes for appetizers, side dishes and desserts. The wedding was a tremendous success and the idea to turn these recipes into a book jelled when I realized exactly how many new and exciting recipes I'd collected and that each new pareve recipe I had tried was better than the last.

Most families (unless they are the strictest of vegetarians) don't eat entirely pareve meals with any frequency. But everyone I know who keeps kosher is always searching for and trying to create pareve dishes that are tasty and classy enough to serve company or present at a *Kiddush*. It's a well-known fact that good pareve recipes are as precious as gold and the best of the best are passed from mother to daughter with the promise to pass them on to future generations. These are the kinds of recipes I wanted for *Perfectly Pareve*.

With *Perfectly Pareve*, the days when pareve meant a snack or a side dish, but never ever a main dish are gone. The sky's now the limit in terms of creative pareve possibilities. By using the increasingly expanding variety of dairyless and meat-free products that simulate their dairy and meat counterparts, you can now make pareve "cream sauces," "cheese cakes" and "cream soups" that are almost indistinguishable from the real thing.

I have stayed away from recipes using tofu or fish. There are already enough cookbooks out there that focus on them. I've also tried to limit myself to the ingredients that the reader can readily find.

*Perfectly Pareve* makes it easy for you to create great-tasting pareve dishes. So when your family and friends start raving about how marvelous a cook you are, don't tell them that what they're eating is actually PAREVE. They'll never believe it. Just smile, pass a second (or third) helping of whichever recipe you've created and take a well-deserved bow.

# Substitutions

| | |
|---|---|
| 1 teaspoon allspice | ½ teaspoon cinnamon, plus ⅛ teaspoon ground cloves |
| 1 teaspoon baking powder | 1 teaspoon baking soda, plus 1 teaspoon cream of tartar |
| 1 cup buttermilk | 1 cup minus 1 tablespoon non-dairy creamer, plus 1 tablespoon lemon juice. Stir together and let stand 5 minutes.<br><br>OR<br><br>1 cup minus 2 teaspoons soy milk, plus 2 teaspoons white vinegar. Stir together and let stand 5 minutes.<br><br>NOTE: This does NOT work for baking when buttermilk is the only liquid used. If you must use it for baking: add 1 egg white for each 1 cup used. |
| 1 square unsweetened chocolate | 3 tablespoons cocoa, plus 1 tablespoon margarine |
| 1½ cups corn syrup | 1 cup sugar, plus ½ cup water |
| 1 tablespoon cornstarch | 2 tablespoons all-purpose flour<br><br>OR<br><br>4 teaspoons quick-cooking tapioca |

| | |
|---|---|
| 1 whole egg | 2 egg yolks, plus 1 tablespoon water<br><br>OR<br><br>2 egg whites<br><br>OR<br><br>¾ cup egg substitute |
| 1 cup all-purpose flour | 1 cup, plus 2 tablespoons cake flour<br><br>OR<br><br>¼ cup matzah cake meal<br><br>OR<br><br>¾ cup potato starch |
| 1 cup cake flour | 1 cup minus 2 tablespoons all-purpose flour |
| 1 clove garlic | ⅛ teaspoon dried garlic powder<br><br>OR<br><br>¼ teaspoon dried minced garlic |
| 1 tablespoon raw ginger | ⅛ teaspoon ginger powder |
| 1 tablespoon fresh herbs | 1 teaspoon dried herbs |
| ⅔ cup honey | 1 cup sugar, plus ⅓ cup water |
| 1 teaspoon Italian seasoning | ¼ teaspoon each of oregano, basil, thyme, rosemary, plus dash of cayenne |
| 1 teaspoon lemon juice | ½ teaspoon vinegar |
| 1 teaspoon mustard powder | 1 tablespoon prepared mustard |
| 1 small onion | 1 tablespoon instant minced onion |
| 1 teaspoon oregano | 1 teaspoon marjoram |

| | |
|---|---|
| ½ cup raisins | ½ cup cut dried prunes |
| 1–3 drops tabasco sauce | dash of cayenne pepper |
| 1 cup canned tomatoes | 1⅓ cups fresh tomatoes simmered 10 minutes |
| 1 cup tomato juice | ½ cup tomato sauce, plus ½ cup water |
| 1 teaspoon Worcestershire sauce | 1 teaspoon bottled steak sauce |
| 1 compressed cake yeast | 1 package OR 2 teaspoons active dry yeast |

# Important Notice

This very special cookbook contains several recipes that call for ingredients which may carry kashrut certification in some communities, but not in others. Please be sure to check all labels to ensure that each item meets with your kashrut standards.

Also, many of these recipes call for the use of various fruits, vegetables, herbs, grains and beans. Because of the halachic obligation to examine such foods for the presence of worms and insects, readers should consult with their local Rabbinical authority regarding the proper procedure to follow when checking them. This is not discussed within the framework of the individual recipes.

# Appetizers

Celebrating at home with family and good food can be the ultimate in fun. It takes a little planning and work, but it can become the kind of event that will be memorable to your relatives for years.

Remember, food can make or break such a get–together and the first thing you serve, those tantalizing appetizers, sets the tone. If you're serving a light meal, or only snacks, keep the preparation simple. For something different, try incorporating the making of the appetizers as part of the overall activities. Nothing makes entertaining more fun than watching a family (with various degrees of skill and knowledge) trying to cook together.

# Vegetable Pot Stickers

A spectacular treat for the eye and tongue.

Makes 35 to 40 pieces.

*¾ cup finely shredded carrots*
*½ cup chopped bean sprouts*
*1¼ cups shredded green cabbage*
*½ cup chopped green onions*
*2 teaspoons chopped ginger root*
*1 teaspoon sesame oil*
*¼ teaspoon white pepper*
*1 large red bell pepper, finely chopped*
*1 egg white*
*1 package round wonton skins*
*Water*
*½ cup oil*
*2 cups vegetable broth*
*1½ tablespoons soy sauce*

In a large bowl, mix together well the carrots, bean sprouts, cabbage, green onions, ginger, sesame oil, pepper, red pepper and egg white. Brush the top of each wonton skin with water. Center 1 tablespoon of the vegetable mixture on top of each wonton skin, fold each skin in half over the vegetable mixture and press the edges together. In a skillet, heat about ¼ of the oil over medium heat. Fry 10 – 12 pot stickers at a time, about 3 minutes each side or until light brown. Stir in ½ cup of the broth and 1 teaspoon of the soy sauce. Cover and cook 5 minutes. Uncover and cook 1 minute longer or until the broth has evaporated. Repeat 3 times with the remaining pot stickers, oil, broth and soy sauce.

# Sweet Potato Spears

So elegant, so different, so easy.

Bake at 400° for 20 minutes.
Makes 12 servings.

*6 medium sweet potatoes, about 4 pounds*
*3 tablespoons olive oil*
*1 teaspoon ground ginger*
*1 teaspoon ground cumin*
*1 teaspoon salt*
*¼ teaspoon black pepper*
*Cooking spray*

Peel the sweet potatoes and cut lengthwise into quarters. Cut each quarter lengthwise into 2 wedges no wider than ¾ inch (2 cm). Toss with oil. Combine the ginger, cumin, salt and pepper and toss with the sweet potatoes. Line a cookie sheet with foil; coat the foil with cooking spray. Arrange the wedges in single layer on a baking sheet and roast 10 minutes, or until the bottoms are lightly browned. Turn the wedges over and brown 10 minutes longer. Potatoes should be tender when pricked with a fork.

NOTE: This can be made a day ahead and reheated. To reheat, place in a 350° oven 5 – 7 minutes.

# Quickie Egg Foo Yung

This is perfect when you crave
Chinese food.

Makes 4 servings.

*1 package fried rice mix*
*6 eggs, separated*
*1 tablespoon soy sauce*
*½ teaspoon salt*
*Dash pepper*
*2 cups bean sprouts*
*¼ cup sliced green onions*

***Sauce**:*
*2 tablespoons cornstarch*
*2 tablespoons soy sauce*
*¼ teaspoon minced garlic*
*2 cups water*

Prepare fried rice according to the package and set aside. With an electric mixer beat together the egg whites, 1 tablespoon soy sauce, salt and pepper and set aside. Beat the egg yolks, together with the cooked fried rice, bean sprouts and green onions. Stir the vegetable mixture into the egg white mixture. Drop ¼ cup mixture per patty onto a greased griddle. Cook and brown on each side.

To make the sauce, combine the cornstarch, 2 tablespoons soy sauce, garlic and water in a saucepan. Simmer, stirring constantly, until thick. Place 2 or 3 patties on a plate and spoon the sauce over them. This recipe can be doubled or tripled.

OPTION: These patties can be made smaller and served without the sauce as a pass-around appetizer.

# Fried Wonton

The perfect use for the
left-over potatoes we've all had
at one time or another.

Makes 60 to 70.

*1 diced onion*
*1 teaspoon minced garlic*
*1 tablespoon oil*
*1 cup mashed potatoes (instant,*
*prepared is okay)*
*1 cup frozen chopped spinach, defrosted*
*and drained*
*Salt and pepper to taste*
*2 packages wonton skins*
*Oil for frying*

In a skillet, sauté the onion and garlic in the 1 tablespoon of oil. When they are soft, remove them from the heat, add the mashed potatoes, spinach, salt and pepper and mix well. Center a tablespoon of the potato mixture on top of a wonton skin. Fold into a triangle, sealing the edges with a little water. Fill and fold the remaining wonton skins. Fry the wontons in about an inch (2½ cm) of oil until brown; carefully, as they cook quickly. Drain on paper towels.

TIP: For extra light and creamy mashed potatoes, add 1 teaspoon baking powder to the potatoes before mashing and then beat them vigorously.

NOTE: These may be made ahead, frozen on cookie sheets and then stored in plastic bags. Defrost and heat in the oven at 350° when ready to use.

# Olivada Crostini

Olives, olives and more olives!

Bake at 350° for 7-10 minutes.
Makes 4 servings.

*3 cups pitted olives, drained*
*3 tablespoons olive oil*
*2 tablespoons toasted pine nuts*
*2 teaspoons minced garlic*
*Salt and pepper to taste*
*1 loaf French bread, sliced on diagonal,*
*10 – 12 slices*
*1 red bell pepper, roasted and sliced*
*Cracked peppercorns*

In a food processor or blender, process the olives, olive oil, pine nuts and garlic until you get a chunky paté. Season to taste with salt and pepper. Preheat oven. Arrange the bread slices in a single layer on a baking sheet. Bake until lightly toasted. Remove toast from the oven and spread with the olive paté. Decorate with roasted bell pepper and sprinkle with a dash of cracked pepper.

### To roast a pepper:

Cut the peppers in ½ and place the cut side down on a greased cookie sheet. Broil until the skin is blackened (2 – 4 minutes), then immediately place the peppers in a paper bag. Let sit for ½ hour. Remove and peel.

DAIRY OPTION: Shred 1 cup mozzarella cheese and sprinkle on top of the peppers. Return the crostini to the oven for an additional 1 minute to slightly melt the cheese and serve hot.

NOTE: The paté can be made 1 week ahead of time; simply store covered in the refrigerator until it is needed.

# Almond and Tomato Tapenade

Sounds difficult...but isn't!
Serve with French bread,
pita, crackers, or fresh vegetables.

Makes about 2 cups.

*2 cups sun-dried tomatoes*
*Hot water for reconstituting tomatoes*
*⅓ cup water*
*1 cup sliced black olives*
*3 tablespoons olive oil*
*1 tablespoon dried basil*
*1 tablespoon lemon juice*
*2 teaspoons minced garlic*
*⅔ cup whole almonds, toasted then ground*
*Salt to taste*

In a small bowl, cover the tomatoes with hot water and let them sit for 15 minutes. Drain the tomatoes and place them in a food processor with the remaining ingredients, except the almonds and salt. Process until almost smooth, pulsing on and off (you can use a blender if you prefer). Add almonds and process on and off for about 1 minute. Season with salt. Serve at room temperature.

NOTE: Store covered in the refrigerator; will keep up to 1 week.

4

# Mushroom Almond Paté

Easy, elegant and luscious.

Makes 1½ cups.

2 tablespoons margarine
1 small onion, chopped
1 teaspoon minced garlic
1½ cups sliced mushrooms
½ teaspoon tarragon
1 cup blanched whole almonds
1 tablespoon lemon juice
2 teaspoons soy sauce
Dash white pepper
Slivered almonds, fresh parsley sprigs,
pimento strips and/or sweet red pepper
strips for garnish

In a large skillet, melt the margarine. Sauté the onion, garlic and mushrooms until tender but not brown; add the tarragon and stir until softened. Let cool for 10 minutes. In a food processor, combine this mixture with the remaining ingredients and process until smooth. Spoon into a serving bowl. Garnish with slivered or finely chopped almonds, fresh parsley sprigs, pimento, or sweet red pepper strips, if you wish. This dish can be doubled and may be frozen.

OPTIONS: Substitute other vegetables, e.g., broccoli for the mushrooms, or whole pecans for the almonds; vary the flavor by using other seasonings such as basil, oregano, dill weed, curry powder or nutmeg.

DAIRY: For a more spreadable consistency, add 2 tablespoons cream cheese, Kefir cheese or Neufchatel cheese.

# Hot Olive Spread

Serve with chips, rye bread, pita or bagel chips.

Makes 2 cups.

1½ cups pitted black olives
3 hard-boiled eggs
1 tablespoon minced parsley
1 teaspoon minced garlic
¼ cup olive oil
3 dashes red-hot-chili sauce (more, if you like)
1 grated hard-boiled egg

In a food processor or blender, combine all the ingredients (except the grated egg) and process to a smooth paste. Spoon into a serving dish, sprinkle with the grated egg and serve.

TIP: Eggs that you have accidentally cracked in the carton can be hard-boiled right away, wrapped in aluminum foil that has been twisted closed at both ends.

# Western Caviar

A tasty treat for the brave of heart.
Serve with tortilla chips.

*2 10-ounce cans black eyed peas, drained*
*2 10-ounce cans hominy, 1 white, 1 yellow,*
*drained*
*½ cup sliced black olives, drained*
*¼ cup sliced jalapeno peppers, drained*
*1 cup chopped green or red bell pepper*
*1 cup chopped green onions*
*3 chopped fresh tomatoes*
*18-ounce bottle Italian salad dressing*

Drain and rinse well all the black-eyed peas, hominy, black olives and jalapenos. Combine the ingredients in a bowl and refrigerate. Marinate overnight.

# South of the Border Dip

This is sort of like a
Mexican vacation for your mouth.
Serve with corn or potato chips.
Also great with vegetables or pita.

Makes 2 cups.

*1 tablespoon chili powder*
*1 teaspoon ground cumin*
*1½ cups canned pinto beans, drained*
*⅓ cup tomato paste*
*3 tablespoons lime juice*
*1 tablespoon water*
*1 tablespoon minced jalapeno pepper*
*1 tablespoon minced coriander*
*2 teaspoons minced garlic*
*¼ teaspoon salt*
*¼ teaspoon freshly ground black pepper*
*¼ cup chopped green bell pepper*
*¼ cup chopped red bell pepper*

In small skillet, over very low heat, heat the chili powder and cumin until just fragrant, about 1 minute. Place the spices into a food processor or blender and add the beans, tomato paste, lime juice, water, jalapeno pepper, coriander, garlic, salt and black pepper. Process until smooth. Add the bell peppers and pulse several times until just chunky-smooth. Pour into a serving dish and chill.

# Crazy Curry Dip

Spicy, so watch out!
Great with vegetables.

Makes 2½ cups.

*2 cups mayonnaise (low-fat varieties work
very well)*
*1 tablespoon ketchup*
*1 tablespoon honey*
*1 tablespoon grated onion*
*¼ teaspoon minced garlic*
*¼ cup grated carrots*
*1½ teaspoons curry powder*
*2 hard-boiled eggs, grated*
*Dash salt*
*7 drops Hot Sauce (or cayenne pepper sauce)*

In a food processor or blender, process all the ingredients very well until smooth. Refrigerate several hours before serving.

DAIRY OPTION: Substitute 1 cup sour cream or plain yogurt for 1 cup of the mayonnaise. Low- and non-fat varieties of sour cream and yogurt can be used as well.

TIP: If an egg cracks while it is boiling, lower the heat and pour a lot of salt on the crack. This will seal the egg, keeping the egg white from leaking into the water.

# Herbed White Bean Dip

Exceptional change
from the ordinary
"sour cream and onion stuff."

Makes 2 cups.

*2 cups canned white kidney beans, drained*
*2 teaspoons dried parsley*
*1 tablespoon fresh lemon juice*
*1 teaspoon minced garlic*
*1 teaspoon olive oil*
*½ teaspoon ground cumin*
*¼ teaspoon dried oregano*
*Salt and black pepper to taste*
*Dash cayenne pepper*
*Cayenne pepper and oregano for garnish*

Purée the beans, parsley, lemon juice, garlic, olive oil, cumin and oregano in a food processor or blender until smooth. Season with salt, black pepper and cayenne pepper. Add additional oregano if needed. Spoon the dip into a serving bowl, cover and chill. Let stand 30 minutes at room temperature before serving. Sprinkle with additional cayenne pepper and oregano to garnish.

NOTE: This can be made 2 days ahead of time.

## Black Bean Dip

A basic dip that you can make
in about a minute.
Serve with chips and salsa
and chunks of avocado.

Makes 2 cups.

2 cups black beans (drain and reserve
liquid)
1 small onion, quartered
2 cloves garlic
¼ teaspoon liquid smoke
2 tablespoons red wine
1 teaspoon salt
1 tablespoon lemon juice

Process all the ingredients in a
blender or food processor until
smooth. If the dip is too think, thin
with some of the liquid from the
beans. Chill for at least 2–3 hours.
Take out of the refrigerator ½ hour
before serving.
NOTE: This will keep for a week or so
in the refrigerator.

## Red Bean Presto Dip

Fast!
Great with toasted pita
or bagel chips.

Makes 1½ cups.

1 cup canned red kidney beans, drained
¼ cup walnuts
1 minced chili pepper
2 minced garlic cloves
¼ cup water
½ cup vegetable oil
1½ teaspoons cider vinegar
½ teaspoon paprika
½ teaspoon ground pepper
¼ teaspoon chili powder
¼ teaspoon salt
¼ teaspoon cumin
Dash Tabasco sauce

In a food processor, combine the
beans, walnuts, chili pepper and
garlic and process for 30 seconds.
While the machine is running, slowly
add the water and oil through the feed
tube. Add the remaining ingredients
and process until smooth. Adjust seasonings to taste. This can be doubled
or tripled.

# Mock Sour Cream

Perfect for a baked potato,
or as a topping for soups and dips.
Much smoother
than the pre-made variety.

Makes 1 cup.

*1 tablespoon margarine*
*1 tablespoon cornstarch*
*1 cup non-dairy creamer*
*1 tablespoon white vinegar*

In a saucepan, melt the margarine over low heat. Remove from the heat and stir in the cornstarch until the mixture is smooth. Add about 2 tablespoons of the creamer and beat with a spoon until smooth. Return to low heat and gradually add the rest of the creamer. Continue cooking and stirring until the mixture comes to a boil. Lower the heat and continue stirring until the mixture becomes the consistency of custard. Remove from the heat, add vinegar and mix well. Cool. This recipe can be doubled.

NOTE: This "sour cream" should NOT be use as a baking substitute for sour cream. It will break down while cooking and you'll end up with a disaster.

# Tofu Cream Cheese

Great for flavored spreads or dips.

Makes about 1 cup.

*1 package silken firm tofu, drained*
*1 tablespoon fresh (only) lemon juice*
*1 tablespoon vegetable oil*
*¼ teaspoon salt*

Drain the tofu over a large bowl. Combine the tofu with the remaining ingredients in a food processor and blend until smooth. Transfer to a container with an airtight lid and refrigerate until cold.

NOTE: Keep in the refrigerator for up to 3 days, after which it tends to break down. It may need to be stirred before using. DON'T use for baking. (Only bake with commercial brands, as they contain stabilizers to hold the ingredients together.)

# Eggplant Dip with Mayonnaise

Simple, easy and tasty but just different enough to make it special.

Makes 6 servings.

*2 eggplants*
*¼ cup diced black olives*
*1 finely chopped onion*
*2 teaspoons minced garlic*
*Juice of one lemon*
*4 tablespoons mayonnaise*
*Salt and pepper to taste*
*Green onions, sliced thin for garnish*
*Black olives, pitted and sliced for garnish*

Grill the eggplants or bake them in the oven for approximately 30 – 40 minutes, until brown outside and very soft inside. Let cool. Scoop out the pulp of the eggplant and purée in a food processor. Pour the purée into a large glass bowl; add the black olives, onion, garlic, lemon juice and mayonnaise and mix well. Season to taste with salt and pepper. Garnish with green onions and black olives and serve.

# Thirst Quenchers

There is nothing quite like a cold drink of water when you're thirsty and lemonade is perfect when the temperature hits the 90s. And let's not forget that the coziest drink on a cold winter's day is hot chocolate. If you're lucky enough to have some whipped cream at home as well, it's wonderful even if you're all alone.

Beverages can quench your thirst, warm your heart, round out a meal, provide a quick pick-me-up and add pizazz to any social occasion.

Fruits and fruit juices added to drinks are good for you. They don't have the additives and dyes that sodas and powdered drinks do. That's why I've tried to incorporate as many fresh fruits and juices in this section as I could. Don't get me wrong; I love Coca Cola® just as much as the next guy, but it can get boring after a while.

# Choose-a-Color Daiquiris

———🍸———

Look great and taste even better.

Makes 4–5 servings.

*⅔ cup frozen lemonade concentrate*
*⅓ cup frozen limeade concentrate*
*⅔ cup light rum*
*¼–⅓ cup powdered sugar*
*3 cups ice cubes*
*Lime or lemon wedges (optional)*

### White Daiquiris:

In a blender, combine the lemonade and limeade concentrates, rum and powdered sugar; cover and whip until smooth. While the blender is running, add the ice cubes, one at a time, through the lid opening, blending until the mixture is slushy. Pour into glasses. Top with lime or lemon slice.

### Red Daiquiris:

Prepare as for White Daiquiris, except use one 6-ounce can of frozen lemonade or limeade concentrate and blend the ingredients with 2 cups frozen unsweetened strawberries or lightly sweetened red raspberries. Garnish with fresh strawberries. Makes 6 servings.

### Blue Daiquiris:

Prepare as for White Daiquiris, except blend ¼ cup blue Curacao liqueur with the frozen lemonade and limeade concentrates, light rum and powdered sugar. Garnish with star fruit or kiwi slices. Makes 6 servings.

### Nonalcoholic Daiquiris:

Prepare as for White Daiquiris, except omit the sugar and substitute ¾ cup unsweetened pineapple juice for the rum. If desired, garnish with a fresh pineapple spear.

# Mock Champagne

———🍸———

Appropriate for any celebration.

Makes 6 servings.

*⅔ cup sugar*
*⅔ cup water*
*½ cup orange juice*
*1 cup grapefruit juice*
*3 tablespoons grenadine syrup*
*4 cups ginger ale, chilled*

In a saucepan, combine the sugar and water. Heat over a low flame and stir until the sugar is dissolved. Bring to a boil and boil for 10 minutes. Cool. Place the orange juice and grapefruit juice in a pitcher and mix in the sugar syrup. Chill thoroughly for at least one hour. Mix in the grenadine and chilled ginger ale just before serving.

TIP: If citrus fruits are warmed in the oven for a few minutes, they will become juicier.

# Banana Slush Punch

Great for any kind of celebration (like *sheva berachos* or an engagement) where you have a lot of people to feed and you don't want to serve soda pop or liquor. This makes plenty of punch, so bring out the big bowl that your great-aunt Sophie left you.

Makes 25–30 servings.

*5 bananas*
*1 12-ounce can frozen orange juice concentrate*
*1 6-ounce can frozen lemonade concentrate*
*2 cups sugar*
*6 cups pineapple juice*
*Water*
*2 2-quart bottles (2-liter) lemon lime soda, chilled*

**P**urée the bananas in a food processor or blender (or mash them thoroughly in a large bowl) and mix with the slightly-thawed frozen juices. Add the sugar and pineapple juice and stir well to dissolve the sugar. Pour into a one-gallon container and add enough water to come within one inch from the top. Refrigerate until you are ready for the punch. When you're ready to serve, pour the basic mixture into a punch bowl and stir in the lemon lime soda.

NOTE: You can freeze the punch base until you're ready to use it. Keeps in the freezer for 3 months.

# Cucumber Cocktail

Sounds weird, but tastes great!

Makes 4 servings.

*1 sliced kiwi*
*2 cups diced cucumber*
*¼ cup water*
*1 tablespoon lemon juice*
*Dash salt*
*1 cup finely chopped ice*

**M**ix all of the ingredients in a blender and process them until smooth.

# Sparkling Fruit Daiquiris

Makes 6–8 servings.

*¾ cup frozen raspberries in light syrup, puréed and poured through a sieve*
*¾ cup frozen banana daiquiri fruit mixer*
*2+ cups ice cubes*
*4 cups lemon- or lime-flavored sparkling water*

**I**n a blender, whip the raspberry purée, fruit mixer and 2 cups ice cubes. Pour into a pitcher and mix in the sparkling water. Serve in ice-filled glasses. This recipe can be doubled or tripled.

# Coffee with a Twist

I am not by nature a coffee drinker. In fact, if I can avoid it, I do. Don't get me wrong; I love the rich, full-bodied aroma of brewing coffee. I just can't get past the bitter taste when I try drinking a cup of it. I've tried adding enough sweeteners to put a normal 5-year-old into sugar shock; still no good. The cream and milk route didn't help either. I was ready to admit defeat until I discovered coffee-flavored drinks.

Okay, so adding ice cream and/or flavoring is cheating a little bit. I guess coffee purists will have to brand me a heretic. But, hot or cold, these beverages hit the spot. They are great after dinner or as a treat when you feel like something a little different. The best part of these recipes is that it only takes a few minutes to put the ingredients together.

HELPFUL TIPS FOR THE FOLLOWING RECIPES

*To make double-strength coffee*: Brew twice as much ground coffee as you normally would, but with the usual amount of cold water. Allow the coffee to cool after brewing. Keep refrigerated in a covered container until you are ready to use it. This coffee can be kept refrigerated for up to one week.

*To make a simple sugar syrup*: Simmer together equal amounts of sugar and water for 5 minutes until the sugar is dissolved. Cool and store indefinitely in a covered jar in the refrigerator.

15

## Café Olé

While I always love the aroma of coffee, I never like the taste. However, when coffee is blended like this, with cocoa and sugar, you can savor its richness without the usual bitterness.

Makes 4 servings.

*4 cups brewed coffee*
*¾ cup firmly-packed brown sugar*
*¼ cup unsweetened cocoa*
*2 teaspoons ground cinnamon*
*Sweetened, non-dairy whipped topping*

Stir the brown sugar, cocoa and cinnamon into the hot coffee; blend well to dissolve. Pour into individual mugs and dollop with whipped topping. Can be doubled.

## Whipped Spiced Coffee

I save the coffee leftover from several of the pots my husband brews (I freeze it in ice cube trays) and whip this up when friends stop by.

Makes 2 servings.

*1 cup double-strength coffee, cold*
*¼ teaspoon cinnamon*
*¼ teaspoon nutmeg*
*1 teaspoon vanilla extract*
*1 cup pareve vanilla ice cream*

Combine all of the ingredients in a blender and mix on high speed for about 30 seconds. Pour into glasses. Sprinkle on top with extra nutmeg or cinnamon. This recipe can be doubled or tripled.

## Banana-Rama

This is so good
you won't want to share it.

Makes 2 servings.

*½ ripe banana, cut into 4 pieces*
*2 tablespoons chocolate syrup*
*1½ cups pareve vanilla ice cream*
*¾ cup double-strength coffee*
*1 teaspoon almond extract*
*Chocolate shavings for garnish*

Combine all of the ingredients in a blender and whip on high speed for 30–40 seconds or until smooth. Pour into glasses and top with chocolate shavings. Can be doubled or tripled.

## Orange Creme Twister

The coffee gives this a rich,
full flavor.

Makes 2 servings.

*2 cups double-strength coffee*
*½ teaspoon orange extract*
*½ cup orange juice*
*1 cup pareve vanilla ice cream*
*Orange peel for garnish*

In a blender whip all of the ingredients, except the orange peel, at high speed until smooth. Pour into glasses and garnish with orange peel. This recipe can be doubled.

# Chocolate Raspberry Creme Cooler

If you can't have a chocolate shake,
this is the next best thing.
It's perfect on a hot, summer,
Shabbos afternoon.

Makes 1 serving.

*1 cup double-strength coffee*
*1 tablespoon raspberry syrup*
*2 tablespoons chocolate syrup*
*¾ cup non-dairy creamer*
*1 cup ice cubes (about 6 cubes)*
*Non-dairy whipped topping*
*Fresh or frozen raspberries for garnish*

Combine the coffee and syrups in a tall glass. Stir until the chocolate is dissolved. Add the non-dairy creamer and stir until blended. Add the ice cubes and top with whipped topping and raspberries. This can be doubled or tripled.

TIP: Iced tea and coffee are improved if the ice cubes are made of tea and coffee.

# Bread, Muffins & Biscuits

**W**hile nowadays, we tend to settle for the prepackaged, store-bought stuff, let's face it — there's nothing quite like the smell, taste and satisfaction that comes from homemade bread.

Making bread is far easier than most people think. You simply need to follow a few easy guidelines.

First, yeast is not the enemy. It's really not difficult to use once you realize that the temperature of the water used to activate the yeast should be between 105–115°F. If it's cooler or hotter, you run the risk of not activating it.

Letting the dough rise twice is also a must. The dough needs the chance to form gluten (important to the structure of the bread) and letting it rise twice lets this happen.

The following recipes are simple and straightforward and make GREAT breads.

# Bread Baking Tips

*IT DIDN'T RISE!* You may have forgotten the yeast, or killed it if you dissolved it in water hotter than 120°F. If you are using a food processor, it may overheat the dough and kill the yeast. Don't throw the dough away. Start a new batch, using 1½ times the required yeast and then knead the old and the new doughs together by hand. There will be plenty of active yeast cells for both loaves.

*IT'S RISING TOO MUCH!* The danger here is that it will collapse when the heat of the oven forces it to rise even more. Just punch the dough down, reshape and let it rise again. Keep a careful eye on it this time, so that it doesn't go beyond the recommended volume.

*THE SIDES AND BOTTOM ARE TOO LIGHT!* This may happen even if the top crust is golden brown. Shiny aluminum pans can be the culprit as they reflect heat rather than absorb it. Return the loaves to the oven, without their pans, for 5 minutes. High gluten flour also develops a nicer crust.

*I'M NOT GETTING THE KIND OF CRUST I WANT!* If it is not thick or crusty enough, place a pie pan of water on the bottom of your oven to generate some steam; placing a baking stone or tiles under the pan may also help. If the crust seems too hard and crispy, let the bread sit in a plastic bag overnight; this works especially well with warm bread.

## French Onion Bread

Bake at 375° for 30–35 minutes.
Makes 2 loaves.

*5–5½ cups all-purpose flour*
*¼ cup onion soup mix*
*3 tablespoons sugar*
*2 teaspoons salt*
*2 packages dry yeast*
*2 tablespoons melted shortening*
*2 cups warm water (120–130°F)*
*1 egg white*
*1 tablespoon water*

Combine 2 cups flour, the soup mix, sugar, salt and yeast in a large bowl; mix well. Add the shortening and warm water and beat at medium speed with an electric mixer for about 3 minutes. Gradually stir in enough of the remaining flour to make a stiff dough.

Turn the dough onto a floured surface and knead until smooth and elastic (about 3 minutes). Place into a well-greased bowl, turning to grease top and sides. Cover and let rise in a warm place (85°F), free from drafts, 1 hour or until doubled in bulk.

Punch dough down; turn onto a lightly floured surface and knead lightly 4 or 5 times. Divide dough in half and roll each portion into a 14x5-inch rectangle. Roll up the dough lengthwise, starting at long side, pressing firmly to eliminate any air pockets; pinch the seam and ends to seal. Place dough, seam side down, on a greased baking sheet and cover.

Let rise in a warm place, free from drafts, 45 minutes or until doubled in bulk. Using a sharp knife, make 3 or 4 slits, about ½-inch deep, diagonally across the loaves. Beat together the egg white and 1 tablespoon water until blended; brush gently over the loaves. Bake until loaves sound hollow when tapped.

TIP: Fresh bread will retain its shape if sliced with a hot knife.

## Zucchini Bread 1

This is a great way to use some of the summer's extra bounty and the extra loaves freeze well.

Bake at 350° for 1 hour.
Makes 2 loaves.

*3 large eggs*
*2 cups sugar*
*1 cup vegetable oil*
*2 cups grated zucchini*
*2 cups all-purpose flour*
*1½ teaspoons baking soda*
*¾ teaspoon baking powder*
*1 teaspoon salt*
*1 teaspoon cinnamon*
*1½ teaspoons vanilla*
*1 cup chopped nuts*
*1 cup raisins (optional)*

Preheat oven. In a large bowl, mix all of the ingredients together. Divide this thick batter into 2 greased 8- or 9-inch loaf pans. Bake; cool 10–15 minutes before removing from pans. DO NOT double this recipe.

## Zucchini Bread 2

Just as good as the other recipe but the apricots add a little zip.

Bake at 350° for 50 minutes.
Makes 2 loaves.

*1 cup coarsely ground walnuts*
*2 cups all-purpose flour*
*2 teaspoons baking soda*
*½ teaspoon baking powder*
*3 eggs*
*1½ cups sugar*
*1 cup vegetable oil*
*2 tablespoons vanilla*
*2 cups zucchini, finely grated*
*½ cup chopped apricots*

Preheat oven. In a bowl, mix together the dry ingredients; set aside. In another bowl, combine the remaining ingredients, except the zucchini and apricots; mix well. Combine the 2 mixtures, add the zucchini and apricots and mix well. Pour into greased loaf pans or 1 square 8- or 9-inch pan and bake (start checking for doneness after about 40 minutes). This recipe can be doubled.

## Blender Quick Orange Bread

This goes fast so you may need to make a double batch.

Bake at 350° for 45–50 minutes.
Makes 1 loaf.

*1 unpeeled seedless orange*
*½ cup orange juice (fresh-squeezed is best)*
*2½ cups all-purpose flour*
*2 teaspoons baking powder*
*2 teaspoons baking soda*
*1 teaspoon pumpkin pie spice*
*½ teaspoon salt*
*1¼ cups sugar*
*2 eggs*
*¼ cup melted margarine*
*½ cup chopped walnuts or pecans*

Preheat oven. Cut the orange into large chunks. In a blender, combine the orange chunks and orange juice and blend until almost smooth; set aside. In a separate bowl, sift together the flour, baking powder, baking soda, pumpkin pie spice and salt. In another bowl, beat sugar, eggs and margarine until smooth. Combine the orange mixture, sugar/egg mixture and dry ingredients and stir just until blended. Fold in the walnuts. Pour into a greased 9x5x3-inch loaf pan. Bake until a toothpick inserted in the center comes out clean. Cool for 10 minutes; remove from pan and cool on a wire rack.

TIP: The leftover rinds of oranges, lemons and grapefruit can be grated and stored for 3 months in an airtight jar in the refrigerator to use in recipes for cakes and frostings.

## Focaccia

Bake at 450° for 20–25 minutes.
Makes 6–8 servings.

*3 cups bread flour*
*2½ teaspoons sugar*
*2½ teaspoons salt*
*1½ cups warm water (105–115°F)*
*2 packages dried yeast*
*¼ cup thinly sliced tomato*
*¼ cup black olives*
*¼ cup thinly sliced red onion*
*Vegetable spray*

In a large bowl, mix well 2½ cups flour, the sugar and salt. Mix the water and yeast in a small bowl and let proof (start to bubble) for 5 minutes. Add the yeast mixture to the flour and mix for about 3 minutes. Gradually stir in enough of the remaining flour to make a semi-stiff dough. Turn dough out onto a lightly floured surface and knead until it is smooth and elastic (about 3 minutes). Place in a well-greased bowl, turning to grease top and sides. Cover and let it rise in a warm place (85°F), free from drafts, 1 hour or until it has doubled in bulk.

Preheat oven. Stretch the dough out (sort of like a pizza in shape) on a greased cookie sheet. Arrange the sliced tomatoes, olives and red onions, on top any way you like. Lightly spray the top with vegetable oil (olive is great!) and bake until golden brown.

TIP: If your bread or cake gets too brown before the inside is cooked, place a pan of water on the oven rack above it before baking.

## Corn Bread Mexicana

This corn bread has a tasty kick that makes you beg for seconds.

Bake at 400° for 30 minutes.
Makes 4–6 servings.

*1 cup whole-wheat flour*
*1 cup cornmeal*
*1½ tablespoons baking powder*
*½ teaspoon chili powder*
*¼ cup honey*
*1 egg*
*2 tablespoons applesauce*
*⅓ cup water*
*¼ cup minced onion*
*¼ cup minced green bell pepper*
*2 tablespoons chopped pimento*
*3 tablespoons chopped green chilies*

Preheat oven. In a bowl, mix the dry ingredients together; set aside. In a larger bowl, mix the honey, egg, applesauce and water; combine with the chopped vegetables and mix well. Add the dry ingredients to wet ingredients and mix. Pour into a lightly oiled or non-stick 8-inch square baking pan.

23

## Cherry Bread

Among my favorite flavors, cherry is second only to chocolate. This bread is one of my top ten.

Bake at 350° for 1 hour.
Makes 8 servings.

*2¼ cups all-purpose flour*
*1 teaspoon double-acting baking powder*
*¾ teaspoon baking soda*
*¼ teaspoon salt*
*1¼ cups sweet canned cherries, drained*
*½ cup coarsely chopped and toasted walnuts*
*½ cup softened margarine*
*¾ cup sugar*
*¼ cup honey*
*2 large eggs*
*⅓ cup fresh orange juice*

Preheat oven. In a large bowl sift together the flour, baking powder, baking soda and salt; set aside. In a second bowl, combine the cherries and the nuts; set aside. In the bowl of an electric mixer, cream the margarine until light and fluffy; gradually add the sugar and honey, beating until it is very light; add the eggs, one at a time. With mixer at its lowest speed, add the flour mixture, reserving ¼ cup, alternating it with the orange juice. Toss the cherry-nut mixture with the reserved flour mixture and fold it into the batter. Turn the batter into a greased and floured loaf pan, approximately 9x5x3 inches. Bake in the center of the oven. Cool for 15 minutes before unmolding the bread onto a cooling rack. When completely cool, wrap it in plastic wrap and keep it a day before serving (it tastes better the second day).

## Mango Bread

Bake at 350° for 1 hour.
Makes 2 loaves.

*2 cups all-purpose flour, sifted*
*2 teaspoons cinnamon*
*2 teaspoons baking soda*
*½ teaspoon salt*
*1¼ cup sugar*
*2 eggs*
*¾ cup vegetable oil*
*2½ cups chopped mango (about 3 large)*
*1 teaspoon lemon juice*
*½ cup raisins*

Combine the first 5 ingredients in a small bowl, set aside. In another small bowl, beat the eggs with oil and add to the flour mixture. Stir in mangoes, lemon juice and raisins. Divide batter into 2 greased 8x4-inch loaf pans and bake until a wooden pick inserted in the center comes out clean.

## Strawberry Bread

This is perfect with a salad and soup
and it freezes well.

Bake at 350° for 35–45 minutes.
Makes 2 loaves.

*3 cups all-purpose flour*
*½ teaspoon salt*
*2 cups sugar*
*1 teaspoon baking soda*
*4 eggs*
*1 cup vegetable oil*
*1 cup chopped walnuts*
*2¼ cups hulled and sliced strawberries*

**P**reheat oven. In a large bowl mix all of the ingredients together. Grease and flour loaf pans; divide the batter evenly between the two. Bake until golden on top. Cool on racks. Do not double this recipe.

## Date Nut Bread

Bake at 350° for 1 hour.
Makes 1 loaf.

*1 cup pitted and finely diced dates*
*1¼ cups cola*
*1 cup firmly packed light brown or*
*granulated sugar*
*2 tablespoons vegetable oil*
*2 cups all-purpose flour*
*1 teaspoon baking powder*
*1 teaspoon baking soda*
*1 egg, well beaten*
*1 teaspoon vanilla extract*
*½ cup chopped pecans or walnuts*

**I**n a small saucepan, heat the cola until it boils. Remove the cola from the heat and stir in dates; mix very well and stir in the sugar and oil. Let cool while preparing the other ingredients. Lightly spoon the flour into a measuring cup. In a mixing bowl, stir together the flour, baking powder and baking soda. Mix thoroughly with the date mixture. Stir in the egg, vanilla and nuts. Pour into a greased and floured 9x5x3-inch loaf pan. Bake until toothpick inserted into the center comes out clean. Cool in its pan, set on a rack, for 20 minutes. Then remove the loaf from the pan and set it on the rack, top side up. When completely cool, wrap it and store overnight before slicing. Makes one loaf.

TIP: To reduce the foam so cola can be accurately measured, use it at room temperature, pour into a large measuring cup and stir rapidly.

# Vegetable Bread

A great way to use the flavor-
and vitamin-packed water
left over from cooking vegetables.

Bake at 350° for 35 minutes.
Makes 1 loaf.

*¾ cup water reserved from steamed
asparagus (or other vegetable), cooled to
100–115°F.
1½ tablespoons vegetable oil
1½ tablespoons honey
½ teaspoon salt
1½ teaspoons yeast
1 tablespoon dried vegetable flakes
2¼ cups bread flour*

In a large bowl, combine the warm vegetable water, oil, honey, salt and yeast and let it start to bubble. Mix in the vegetable flakes and bread flour. Let rise to double in height and then punch down. Roll out on a floured surface and knead for several minutes and then shape the dough into a loaf. Place into a greased loaf pan and let rise for 60–90 minutes. Preheat oven and bake until golden brown on top.

### For a bread machine:

Place ingredients into the machine in the order listed above. Be careful not to let the yeast get wet during the set up or it will activate prematurely.

TIP: To freshen stale breads, sprinkle the crust with cold water and place in an oven, preheated to 350º, for 10 minutes.

# Double Berry Muffins

You can use any type of berry or jam
in this muffin. Whatever berry
is lying around in my refrigerator or
freezer is what ends up in these.

Bake at 400° for 23–25 minutes.
Makes 12 muffins.

*1½ cups all-purpose flour
1 cup oatmeal (any variety, uncooked)
½ teaspoon cinnamon
½ cup sugar
¼ teaspoon salt
1 tablespoon baking powder
1 cup non-dairy creamer
⅓ cup melted margarine
2 egg whites, lightly beaten
1 teaspoon grated lemon peel
¾ cup fresh or frozen blueberries
¼ cup preserves, raspberry or strawberry*

Preheat oven. Line 12 medium muffin cups with paper baking cups or lightly grease the bottoms only. In a bowl, combine the flour, oatmeal, cinnamon, sugar, salt and baking powder. Mix well. Add the non-dairy creamer, margarine, egg whites and lemon peel; mix just until the dry ingredients are moistened. Gently stir in blueberries. Fill muffin cups half full. Spoon 1 teaspoon of preserves over the batter. Spoon remaining batter over the preserves. Bake until golden brown. Let muffins stand a few minutes before you remove them from the pan. Serve warm.

# Morning Glory Muffins

Lots of ingredients, but
easy, easy, easy!

Bake at 350° for 30–35 minutes.
Makes 16 muffins.

*1 cup all-purpose flour*
*1 cup whole-wheat flour*
*2 teaspoons baking soda*
*2 teaspoons ground cinnamon*
*½ teaspoon salt*
*½–¾ cup brown sugar*
*2 cups coarsely grated carrots (about 3-4)*
*¼ cup golden raisins*
*¼ cup dark raisins*
*½ cup chopped pecans*
*½ cup shredded coconut*
*2 teaspoons grated orange rind*
*1 Granny Smith or other tart apple, peeled*
*and grated*
*3 large eggs*
*1 cup vegetable oil*
*1 teaspoon vanilla extract*
*Cinnamon-sugar mixture for topping*

Preheat oven. In a large bowl, sift together the flours, baking soda, cinnamon and salt. Add the brown sugar and mix well. Stir in the carrots, both kinds of raisins, pecans, coconut, orange rind and apples; set aside. In a small bowl, whisk together the eggs, oil and vanilla extract. Add this to the flour mixture, stirring until just combined. Spoon the batter into greased muffin tins (¼-cup size), filling them to the top. Sprinkle the cinnamon-sugar mixture on top. Bake the muffins until they are springy to the touch. Allow to cool for five minutes; turn out onto a rack.

NOTE: When making cinnamon-sugar, the ratio is 1 cup sugar to 1½ teaspoons cinnamon. (Will make more than you need.)

DAIRY OPTION: You can substitute 1 cup plain yogurt for most of the oil, but you will still need to add 2 tablespoons of oil to the mixture.

TIP: Roll dried fruit and nuts in cake flour before using to keep them from sinking to the bottom of a cake.

# Biscuit Quick

As good as the stuff in the box!

Makes 12 biscuits.

*1 cup all-purpose flour*
*1½ teaspoons baking powder*
*½ teaspoon salt*
*1 tablespoon shortening*

In a large bowl, combine all the ingredients and cut in the shortening until it is mixed well. Gather the dough together by kneading it for about 1 minute. Place on a floured surface and roll out to a thickness of about ½ inch. Cut with a 3-inch round cutter. The recipe can be doubled or tripled and used as a substitution for any kind of biscuit mix.

# Sweet Potato Rolls

A non-traditional bread that gets
rave reviews whenever you serve it.
This is also a perfect recipe
to serve with a salad and soup
for a quick meal.

Bake at 400° for 25 minutes.
Makes 36 rolls.

*1½ pounds sweet potatoes, quartered*
*Water*
*2 teaspoons (2 packages) fast rising yeast*
*¼ cup sugar*
*1½ cups margarine, melted*
*1 cup honey*
*¼ cup vegetable oil*
*2 eggs, beaten to blend*
*½ teaspoon salt*
*2 teaspoons all-purpose flour*
*4 cups whole-wheat flour, approximately*
*4 cups graham cracker crumbs*

Boil the potatoes in water until
they are tender, about 20 minutes. Drain, reserving 1 cup of the liquid. Place the potatoes in a
medium-sized bowl. Pour the reserved
liquid into a large bowl; cool to about
120° and then sprinkle the yeast and
sugar over the liquid. If it doesn't dissolve on its own, you can mix it
slightly. Set the yeast mixture aside
until foamy, about 5 minutes. In a
food processor or blender, blend the
potatoes, ½ cup melted margarine, ½
cup honey, oil, eggs and salt until
smooth. Add the potato mixture to
the yeast mixture. Mix well and add in
the all-purpose flour. Gradually stir
in enough whole-wheat flour (½ cup
at a time) to form a soft, slightly
sticky dough.

Turn out onto a lightly floured surface and knead until smooth and elastic, adding more whole-wheat flour if
the dough is too sticky. Lightly oil a
large bowl. Add dough, turning to
coat entire surface. Cover bowl with
kitchen towel. Let dough rise in a
warm, draft-free area until doubled in
volume, about 30 minutes.

Preheat oven. Grease three 9-inch
round cake pans. Punch dough down.
Turn dough onto a lightly floured
surface and knead until smooth. Divide dough into thirds. Cut each third
into 12 pieces. Roll each piece into a
ball.

In a bowl, mix remaining 1 cup
melted margarine and ½ cup honey
until well blended. Dip each dough
ball into honey mixture and then roll
in graham cracker crumbs to coat.
Place the 12 balls in each prepared
pan, arranging close together. Let
stand 10 minutes. Bake until golden
brown.

Rolls can be prepared ahead of time.
Cool completely, wrap tightly and
store in the refrigerator for 1 day or
freeze for up to 1 month. Reheat rolls
before serving. Serve warm.

# Focaccia for the Grill

Italian flatbread made simple and you can whip it up in just a few minutes.

Makes 4 servings.

*1 cup water (l00°–115°F)*
*2 teaspoons instant yeast (see note below)*
*1 tablespoon honey*
*2 tablespoons olive oil*
*2 tablespoons durum semolina or stone ground cornmeal*
*2 cups unbleached bread flour*
*1 teaspoon salt*
*1 cup unbleached all-purpose flour*
*Olive oil cooking spray*

Place water, yeast, honey, olive oil, semolina (or cornmeal) and bread flour in a large bowl or electric mixing bowl using a dough hook. Stir to blend and let rest a few minutes. Stir in salt and then add the remaining all-purpose flour to make a soft dough. Knead with dough hook or by hand to form a soft, but not too sticky dough, about 8-12 minutes. Remove dough from bowl, lightly oil the top of it and allow to rest, covered with a towel for about 45 minutes.

Punch down dough and allow it to rest another 15 minutes before using it in a recipe. Otherwise, you may refrigerate dough in an oiled plastic bag for up to two days.

Flatten dough gently to make it into a generous 15-inch round size. Sprinkle a large, sideless, cookie sheet or a 16-inch aluminum pizza pan or a rectangular baking sheet lightly with semolina or cornmeal. Dimple top of the dough with your fingertips. Drizzle with olive oil, dust with salt and coarse black pepper (shavings of fresh garlic or sautéed onions also work really well).

Preheat the grill to a medium setting. Place the baking sheet or pan on the grill and then lower the grill cover to promote cooking on the dough's top as well as bottom. Allow bread to "set up" (sit out at room temperature) a few minutes. Reduce heat to low and using a metal spatula, ease focaccia directly onto the grill. Bake until done, another 5–8 minutes. If at any time the focaccia seems to be cooking too quickly, reduce heat.

NOTE: If you want this dough for supper and will be out all day, use only ½ teaspoon yeast. Prepare dough, cover (or leave in bread machine) and allow dough a long, leisurely rise throughout the day. Then it's ready when you are.

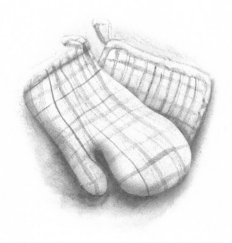

## Herbed Muffins

These outstanding muffins take only
a few minutes to throw together.

Bake at 375° for 18–20 minutes.
Makes 12 muffins.

*2 cups all-purpose flour*
*1 tablespoon sugar*
*2 teaspoons baking powder*
*1 teaspoon garlic powder*
*1 teaspoon dry mustard*
*½ teaspoon salt*
*1 slightly beaten egg*
*1 cup non-dairy creamer*
*½ cup grated carrots*
*¼ cup chopped green onions*
*4 tablespoons mayonnaise*

Preheat oven. In a large bowl, sift
the flour and add the rest of the
dry ingredients; set aside. In a small
bowl, mix the egg with the rest of the
ingredients. Blend the egg mixture
gently into the flour mixture. Spray
the muffin pans with cooking spray
and spoon batter into the muffin
cups.

DAIRY OPTION: You can substitute 4
tablespoons of plain yogurt or sour
cream for the mayonnaise.

# Soups

O n a cold dismal day, soup can be better than hot chocolate! And it is full of vitamins and nutrients. The ready-made stuff is quick and easy, however, it really doesn't have that homemade taste and the powdered stuff in a cup — well, it's got enough salt in it to keep a herd of deer happy throughout the winter.

Anyone can make a soup, but in order to make a good pareve one, you need a super recipe.

Luckily, there are plenty in this chapter to help you along. If you're in a hurry, you can even use a ready-made stock. With these easy-to-make recipes, your guests will be begging for seconds.

# Quick "Cream" Soups

## Makes 4 servings.

*Place into a soup pot:*
*2 cubed potatoes*
*3 cups water (or stock), enough to cover*

ADD
*2 stalks chopped broccoli*
*1 teaspoon minced onion*
*1 pareve bouillon cube*

OR
*2 chopped carrots*
*¼ teaspoon ground ginger*

OR
*1 cup chopped mushrooms*
*2 tablespoons white wine*

OR
*2 chopped celery stalks*
*¼ teaspoon dried tarragon, marjoram or savory*

OR
*1 package frozen spinach*
*dash nutmeg*
*¼ teaspoon lemon juice*

OR
*1 cup corn*
*1 teaspoon dried parsley*

OR
*1 cup peas*
*¼ teaspoon ginger*
*¼ teaspoon cinnamon*
*¼ teaspoon pepper*
*1 teaspoon white vinegar*

OR
*1 chopped sweet potato or ½ cup chopped acorn squash*
*½ teaspoon dried Italian herbs*

Simmer the soup until the vegetables are tender; cool. Purée in blender or food processor until smooth. Add salt/pepper to taste. These amounts can be doubled or tripled.

### To top off soups:

Chopped hard-boiled egg; popcorn; chopped fresh dill, coriander, or basil for tomato-based soups; chopped fresh mint for cold fruit soups; toasted herb bread croutons over onion soups; vegetable purées on top of "creamed" soups (see below).

### Vegetable cream purée:
*½ cup non-dairy whipped topping*
*¼ cup spinach, beets or carrots, etc., cooked thick, puréed, cold*

Fold the cold vegetable purée into the whipped topping. Pipe through a pastry bag into concentric circles over any creamed soup before serving. With a toothpick, draw from the center of circle outward, to create a flower or other design. Very attractive on white, cream-type soups.

### Your very own croutons:

Cube stale bread (I keep the crusts on) and toss with melted margarine to coat well but not make soggy. Season lightly with salt, pepper, garlic powder and paprika. Either sauté in a skillet until golden or spread on a baking sheet and bake at 375°F, turning the cubes until they are golden on all sides. Cool and store in an airtight container.

# Creamy Spinach Soup

This isn't remotely like the spinach your mom tried to get you to eat.

Makes 6 servings.

*1 large onion, coarsely chopped*
*6 cups water*
*3 peeled and chopped potatoes*
*3 medium zucchini, thickly sliced*
*2 tablespoons soy sauce*
*2 cups firmly-packed fresh spinach leaves*
*Freshly ground pepper*
*½ cup sliced mushrooms (optional)*

Place the onion in a large pot with ½ cup of the water. Cook, stirring constantly, until the onion softens slightly, about 3 minutes. Add the remaining water and the potatoes, zucchini and soy sauce and bring to a boil; reduce the heat, cover and simmer for 35 minutes. Add the spinach and pepper and cook for another 2 minutes. Remove from the heat. In a blender, purée the soup in batches and return to the pot; add mushrooms, if desired. Heat gently for 5 minutes. Serve hot.

# Roasted Red Pepper Soup

A sweet and savory soup that is perfect any time of the year.

Makes 6 servings.

*4–5 red bell peppers*
*3 cloves elephant garlic*
*(or 6 cloves regular garlic*)*
*5–6 fresh basil leaves*
*1 tablespoon honey*
*1 cup tomato sauce*
*½ cup tomato purée*
*2 cups vegetable stock*
*Lemon pepper to taste*

Blacken red peppers under your broiler until the skins are charred and shriveled. Bake the elephant garlic at 350°F, leaving the skins on until it's soft and skins are quite dark, but not burned (15-20 minutes). Remove peppers and garlic from oven and place them in a paper bag; fold over the top and leave them in there for about 15 minutes until their skins peel off. Purée peppers and garlic in food processor until thick, but not chunky. Toss in basil leaves and purée.

Transfer the red pepper purée to a stockpot. Add honey, tomato sauce, tomato purée and vegetable stock. Simmer until heated through. Add lemon pepper to season. Adjust the amount of vegetable stock if needed (add more stock for thinner soup). Adjust honey, tomato sauce and basil to taste. This is great garnished with chow mein noodles or croutons.

* If using regular garlic, don't bake it. Sauté it over a low flame in 1 tablespoon olive oil until it's soft.

# Broccoli Potato Soup

This rich soup tastes
like it's made with cream.

Makes 6 servings.

*1 cup chopped onions*
*1 teaspoon minced garlic*
*Salt and pepper to taste*
*¼ teaspoon dried thyme*
*2½ cups vegetable broth*
*1 cup water*
*3 large potatoes, peeled and cubed*
*2 pounds broccoli*
*1 teaspoon fresh lemon juice*

In a large saucepan, sauté the on-ions, garlic, salt, pepper and thyme in 1 cup of the broth, until onions are tender. Stir in the remaining broth and the water and bring to a boil. Add the potatoes and cook until they're fork-tender. Meanwhile, trim the ends and tough parts of the broccoli stalks. Cut the florets and stalks into 1 inch pieces and add to the soup mix-ture. Cook until the broccoli is tender, 8–10 minutes. In a blender or food processor, purée the soup in 2 batches until smooth. Return the soup to the saucepan and add the lemon juice; heat thoroughly and serve. This recipe can be doubled or tripled.

NOTE: I like my soups on the chunky side, so I only purée half of the mix-ture. I also like to sprinkle homemade croutons on top before serving.

# Creamed Potato-Thyme Soup

Anytime is "thyme" for a great soup.
The wine adds a fullness
to the flavor.

Makes 6–8 servings.

*2 tablespoons margarine*
*1 medium onion, minced*
*2 thinly sliced scallions, white part only*
*3 minced shallots*
*2½ cups vegetable stock*
*2 teaspoons finely chopped fresh thyme or*
*tarragon*
*2 cups firmly-packed mashed potatoes*
*¼ cup dry white wine*
*Salt and pepper to taste*
*3 tablespoons chopped fresh chives for*
*garnish (optional)*

In a heavy 2 to 3-quart saucepan, melt the margarine. Saute the on-ion, scallions and shallots, stirring constantly, until the onions are soft but not browned. Stir in the stock and herbs; bring to a boil, stirring occa-sionally. Gradually mix in the pota-toes, a cup at a time; bring to a second boil. Reduce heat to low and stir in the wine; simmer 5 minutes, stirring oc-casionally. Season with salt and pep-per. Serve garnished with chives.

# Vegetable, Bean and Noodle Soup

A great soup for getting kids to eat all the vegetables they refuse to touch otherwise.

Makes 8–10 servings.

*1 large onion, chopped*
*1 large potato, peeled and cubed*
*4 cups vegetable stock or water*
*½ cup celery, cut into ½-inch pieces*
*½ pound green beans, cut into ½-inch pieces*
*¼ head of cabbage, sliced thin*
*1½ cups stemmed and coarsely sliced spinach*
*1 thinly sliced carrot*
*¼ cup chopped red bell pepper*
*1 teaspoon dried or fresh dill*
*2 cups cooked macaroni noodles, well drained*
*1 16-ounce can kidney beans, drained*
*Salt and pepper to taste*
*Cayenne pepper to taste*

In a large soup pot, combine the onion, potatoes and stock and bring the mixture to a boil. Reduce the heat and simmer for 10 minutes. Add the celery, green beans, cabbage, spinach, carrot, red pepper, dill, noodles and kidney beans. Cover and simmer 10 minutes. Season with salt, pepper and cayenne.

DAIRY OPTION: Sprinkle a little parmesan cheese on top of each serving.

# Carrot Soup with Spinach

This simple and delicious soup combines two ingredients — carrots and spinach — that kids will gobble up.

Simmer for 30 minutes.
Makes 6 servings.

*1 pound carrots, scrubbed and cut into 1-inch chunks*
*1 small parsnip, chopped*
*1 small onion, quartered*
*1 celery rib, cut into 2-inch pieces*
*3 cups vegetable stock*
*¼ teaspoons nutmeg*
*Salt and pepper to taste*
*1 cup stemmed spinach leaves*
*1 cup croutons*

Combine the carrots, parsnip, onion, celery and vegetable stock in a heavy saucepan. Cover and bring to a boil. Reduce the heat to low and simmer. Using a slotted spoon, transfer the vegetables to a food processor or blender; purée adding a small amount of cooking liquid to the vegetables. Return the purée to the saucepan together with the stock. Add the nutmeg, salt and pepper. Next, place the spinach in a food processor or blender, add 1 cup of the soup mixture to the spinach and purée. Stir the spinach purée into soup and heat; serve hot with croutons.

# "Cream" of Celery Soup

This is an elegant start to any meal.
My motto: Garlic is welcome
in any amount and at any time!

Makes 6–8 servings.

*12 large celery stalks*
*2 tablespoons vegetable oil*
*1 large onion, chopped*
*¼ cup minced garlic*
*2 tablespoons all-purpose flour*
*3 medium potatoes, peeled and diced*
*Water*
*2 teaspoons Chinese Five Spices*
*2 tablespoons chopped fresh parsley*
*2 tablespoons chopped fresh dill*
*¼ cup celery leaves*
*1–1 ½ cups pareve non-dairy creamer, as needed*
*Salt and freshly ground pepper to taste*
*Chopped fresh dill or parsley for garnish*

Trim 10 stalks of celery and cut them into ½-inch pieces. Trim the remaining 2 stalks, slice them into ¼-inch pieces and set aside. Heat 1 tablespoon of the oil in a soup pot; add the onion and garlic and sauté over medium heat until the onions are golden. Sprinkle in the flour, stirring until it disappears. Add the 10 stalks of celery, the potatoes and just enough water to cover and bring to a simmer. Stir in the seasoning mix, herbs and celery leaves and continue simmering gently until the vegetables are tender, about 25 minutes.

Remove from the heat. With a slotted spoon, transfer the solid ingredients to a food processor or blender and purée in batches until smooth. Stir the purée back into the soup pot. Return to a very low flame and add enough non-dairy creamer to achieve a slightly thick consistency.

Heat the remaining oil in a small skillet, add the reserved celery and sauté over moderate heat until touched with golden spots. Stir the celery into the soup, then season to taste with salt and pepper.

Serve at once, or allow the soup to stand for an hour or so, heating through just before serving. Garnish with chopped dill or parsley. This recipe can be doubled or tripled.

# Wild Rice Soup

This is a nice twist on an old classic.
You can add exotic mushrooms
galore and give it an unusual flavor.

Makes 8–10 servings.

*1 cup pearl barley*
*1 cup wild rice*
*2 chopped onions*
*1 pound halved or quartered mushrooms*
*4 medium potatoes, cubed*
*⅓ cup shredded carrots*
*1 tablespoon dried parsley*
*8–10 cups vegetable broth*

In a large pot, combine all the ingredients. Mix well. Bring to a boil. Reduce flame and cover. Simmer 40–60 minutes and serve.

# Garlic Bean Soup

Don't tell anyone that this only
has 4 ingredients!
They'll never believe you.

Makes 6 servings.

*2½ cups vegetable broth*
*2 tablespoons minced garlic*
*1 chopped onion*
*4 cups cooked white beans (or canned
drained)*

Combine the broth, garlic and onion in a large saucepan (or microwave bowl) and cover. Simmer the
mixture until the onions are soft.
Transfer half the soup to a blender or
food processor; add half the beans and
purée. Return the soup to the pan (or
bowl). Add the remaining beans and
cook until the beans are heated
through. Simmer for 20 minutes on
the stove or 7 minutes in the microwave. This recipe can be doubled or
tripled. Croutons are a wonderful addition.

TIP: When doubling a recipe, don't
automatically double the spices until
you taste things first.

# Cold "Cream" of Pea and Cucumber Soup

Peas that don't taste like peas.

Makes 6–8 servings.

*1 cup chopped onion*
*3 minced garlic cloves*
*2 large potatoes, peeled and diced*
*1 large cucumber, peeled, seeded and
coarsely chopped*
*4 cups water*
*2 cups frozen green peas, thawed*
*¼ cup chopped fresh parsley*
*2 tablespoons chopped fresh dill*
*2 cups non-dairy creamer or soy milk, as
needed*
*Juice of ½–1 lemon, to taste*
*Salt and freshly ground pepper to taste*
*1 cup fresh green peas, lightly steamed*
*1 cup peeled, seeded and finely diced
cucumber*

Combine the onion, garlic, potatoes, cucumber and water in a
soup pot. Simmer gently, covered, until the vegetables are tender, about 25
minutes. Transfer the drained, cooked
vegetables to a food processor or
blender and add the thawed peas,
parsley and dill; purée until very
smooth. Return the purée to the soup
pot and stir in just enough creamer or
soy milk to achieve a slightly thick
consistency. Add lemon juice, salt and
pepper to taste. Let the soup cool to
room temperature, then stir in the
steamed fresh peas and additional cucumber. Serve at room temperature,
or refrigerate for 1–2 hours and serve
chilled.

# Chili and Lentil Soup

This is a versatile kind of soup.
If you cook it long enough
it turns into chili.

Makes 6–8 servings.

*4 cups dried lentils*
*6–7 cups water (or substitute tomato juice*
*for 2 cups)*
*3–4 chopped fresh tomatoes*
*2 teaspoons ground cumin*
*1 teaspoon paprika*
*½ teaspoon dried thyme (or 2 teaspoons*
*fresh thyme)*
*10–12 medium garlic cloves, minced*
*2 medium onions, finely chopped*
*2 teaspoons salt*
*Freshly ground black pepper*
*4–6 tablespoons tomato paste*
*1–2 tablespoons red wine vinegar or*
*balsamic vinegar*
*Crushed red pepper to taste*
*Minced fresh parsley or cilantro*
*for garnish (optional)*

Put lentils and water in large pot and bring them to a boil, then lower heat to a simmer. Partially cover and cook for about 30 minutes, checking to make sure it's JUST simmering. After 30 minutes add the tomatoes, cumin, paprika, thyme, garlic and onions. Stir, cover again and cook for another 45–60 minutes until lentils are tender. Check the water level and add more water or tomato juice if needed. Stir every 10–15 minutes. Add salt, black pepper and tomato paste. Simmer slowly for 30 more minutes, until lentils are very soft. About 10 to 15 minutes before serving, add vinegar and red pepper. Serve with topping, if desired.

NOTE: Can be frozen. Cooks nicely in a crock-pot. Just put in everything but the last two ingredients and cook. Add the last two ingredients right before serving.

# Sweet Carrot Soup

So good it could almost be a dessert.
It is very sweet, so a little
goes a long way.

Makes 6 servings.

*2 cups thickly sliced carrots*
*1½ cups orange juice*
*1 cup apricot nectar*
*¼ cup lemon juice*

Place the carrots in a steamer basket over boiling water. Cover saucepan and steam until carrots are very tender (about 15 minutes). Transfer the carrots to a blender, add the remaining ingredients and purée. Serve chilled or at room temperature.

DAIRY OPTION: Swirl ¼ cup sour cream or yogurt into the soup and serve.

# Creamy Carrot Soup

Croutons add just the right
amount of crunch.

Makes 4 servings.

*2 cups sliced carrots*
*1½ cups pareve chicken broth*
*1 medium onion, coarsely chopped*
*2 tablespoons rice*
*1 pinch grated nutmeg*
*Salt and pepper to taste*
*Grated lemon peel*
*Plain croutons for garnish*

**P**lace all of the ingredients except
the croutons in a medium saucepan. Bring to a boil and then cover.
Reduce the heat and simmer until the
vegetables and rice are tender. Cool
slightly and purée the mixture (in
batches) in a food processor or blender
until smooth. Just before serving, reheat the soup and adjust the seasonings. Garnish with croutons and serve
hot. This recipe can be doubled or tripled. You can also make this a day or
two ahead and then reheat.

# Tomato-Dill Bisque

This very elegant soup
is even more wonderful when
the tomatoes are fresh off the vine.

Makes 5 cups.

*2 medium onions, chopped*
*1 sliced garlic clove*
*2 tablespoons margarine*
*2 pounds peeled and cubed tomatoes*
*½ cup water*
*1 pareve chicken-flavored bouillon cube or*
*1 tablespoon powdered bouillon*
*2¼ teaspoons fresh or ¾ teaspoon dried*
*dill weed*
*¼ teaspoon salt*
*⅛ teaspoon pepper*
*½ cup mayonnaise*
*Dill (fresh or dried) for garnish*

**I**n a 2-quart saucepan over a medium heat, sauté the onions and
garlic in the margarine for 3 minutes.
Add the tomatoes, water, bouillon,
dill, salt and pepper and mix well.
Cover and simmer for 10 minutes. Remove from the heat and cool. Blend
half of the mixture at a time in a
blender or food processor until
smooth. Pour the batches into a large
glass bowl (no metal bowls, to avoid a
chemical reaction between the metal
and the acid from the tomatoes). Stir
in the mayonnaise, making sure that
it's well-blended. Cover and chill overnight. Garnish with the dill.

DAIRY OPTION: Substitute sour
cream or yogurt for the mayonnaise
and serve with a dollop of sour cream
or mayonnaise on top.

# Vegetarian "Chicken" Broth

Adding matzo balls, noodles or rice gives a nice finish to the flavor. You can also use this broth in any recipe that calls for chicken stock.

Simmer 3–4 hours.
Makes 8–10 servings, or approximately 6–7 cups.

*2–3 coarsely chopped onions*
*4–5 thickly sliced carrots*
*4–5 celery stalks, with leaves*
*1–2 thickly sliced parsnips*
*1–2 largely cubed turnips*
*1 largely cubed kohlrabi*
*1 finely diced potato*
*½ cup fresh parsley*
*⅔–1½ cups fresh chopped coriander (cilantro)*
*1–2 tablespoons pareve chicken stock powder*
*Salt and pepper to taste*

Place all the ingredients in a large stock pot and cover with 8–10 cups water. Bring to a boil and then simmer (you may need to add a little water if the level is too low). Strain out the vegetables. At this point you can use the broth as is, or you can purée the strained vegetables and add them to the broth to make it thicker. It can be enjoyed as is, but also is a great stock to use as a basis for other soups.

# Butternut Lentil Soup

Simmer for 30–40 minutes.
Makes 6–8 servings.

*2 chopped celery stalks*
*1 chopped onion*
*1 chopped red pepper*
*1 chopped carrot*
*1 small butternut squash or*
*3–4 cups pumpkin, cubed*
*1 potato, peeled and chopped*
*4 cups vegetable stock*
*½ cup split red lentils*
*Nutmeg to taste*
*Salt and pepper to taste*

In a large soup pot, sauté the celery, onion, red pepper, carrot, squash and potato for about 5 minutes or until the onion has softened. Add the stock and lentils and season lightly. Simmer. Cool slightly and purée (in batches) in a blender or food processor. Reheat and adjust seasoning to taste. Simmer 30–40 minutes. This recipe can be doubled or tripled.

# "Cream" of Corn Soup

This soup is easy to make and great for a cold day in the middle of winter.

Simmer for 30 minutes. Makes 8 servings.

*2½ cups corn*
*1 cup chopped onion*
*2 tablespoons margarine*
*¼–½ cup cornmeal (as thickener)*
*4 cups water*
*½ cup chopped celery*
*Salt to taste*
*Soy sauce to taste*

In a saucepan, sauté the corn and onions in the margarine over a medium heat. Remove the corn and onions from the heat and add cornmeal, stirring until all the veggies are covered. Slowly add water, stirring to avoid lumps. Bring the soup to a boil and simmer. Add the celery and cook 10 more minutes. If the soup is too thick, add more water. Salt and soy sauce can be added at any time during the process. This recipe can be doubled or tripled.

MEAT OPTION: Use chicken stock instead of water.

DAIRY OPTION: Substitute ½ cup of the water with ½ cup cream.

# Hearty Vegetable Soup

This full-bodied soup is a lifesaver when you need to whip something up in less than an hour.

Makes 8–10 servings.

*1 large onion, minced*
*4 tablespoons margarine*
*½ cup diced carrots*
*¾ cup shredded cabbage*
*½ cup peas*
*¼ cup diced string beans*
*¼ cup diced celery*
*⅓ cup whole-kernel corn*
*2 teaspoons chopped dried parsley*
*1 diced parsley root*
*1 diced parsnip*
*1½ cups diced boiled potatoes*
*1 cup canned tomatoes*
*8 cups boiling water*
*1 teaspoon sugar*
*2 teaspoons salt*

In a large pot, sauté the onion in the margarine until it's transparent. Add all of the remaining vegetables, except the potatoes and tomatoes and cook for 10 minutes, stirring constantly. Add potatoes, tomatoes, water and seasonings. Simmer until all of the vegetables are tender (about 15 minutes). Serve hot.

MEAT OPTION: Sauté 1 pound of cut-up stew or stir-fry meat with the onions, drain any fat and continue as directed.

TIP: Chewing gum while peeling onions will prevent tears.

# Chilled Mango Soup

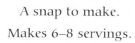

Distinctive and delicious.

Makes 8–10 servings.

*4 very ripe medium mangos*
*2 cups water*
*1 cup sugar*
*4 whole cloves*
*4 star anise*
*1 tablespoon cornstarch, mixed with 2*
*tablespoons water, or 1 tablespoon*
*small-grain tapioca*
*1 cup unsweetened coconut milk*
*3 tablespoons dark rum*
*1 cup chilled white wine*
*Mint sprigs for garnish*

Peel and pit the mangos. Reserve the pulp of half a mango for garnish. Purée the remaining mango pulp in a food processor; set aside. In a medium-sized saucepan, combine the water, sugar, cloves, star anise and cornstarch mixture or tapioca. Bring to a boil. Reduce the heat to medium-low and simmer gently for about 15 minutes, uncovered and stirring often, until the liquid is thick and syrupy. Stir in the puréed mango, coconut milk and rum to the syrup. Cook until the soup just returns to a boil and remove from the heat. Strain the soup through a fine sieve, pressing through the mango pulp; discard all of the large pieces. Cook the soup for 2–3 minutes more and remove from the heat. Stir in the wine and refrigerate until chilled. Dice the reserved mango for the garnish. Pour the soup into 8–10 large wineglasses and garnish with mango and mint sprigs.

# Summer Melon Soup

Distinctive melon soup header decoration

A snap to make.

Makes 6–8 servings.

*6 ripe strawberries*
*3 ripe pears, peeled and chopped*
*3 slices watermelon, cubed*
*½ cantaloupe, cubed*
*½ honeydew melon, cubed*
*½ cup orange juice*
*½ cup cranberry juice*
*¼ cup pineapple juice*
*¼ teaspoon cinnamon*
*1 teaspoon red wine (optional)*
*1 thinly sliced lime for garnish*
*Fresh mint sprigs for garnish*

In a blender or food processor purée in batches all of the fruit, juices, cinnamon and wine; pour into a large bowl and mix well. Refrigerate for at least 2 hours. Ladle the soup into bowls and garnish with lime slices and mint.

DAIRY OPTION: A dollop of whipped cream or sour cream swirled into the soup just before serving looks beautiful.

## Vichyssoise

This recipe is so close to the real thing that it is hard to tell the difference.

Makes 4 cups.

*4 cups water*
*1 pound peeled and diced potatoes*
*2 cups chopped onions*
*6 pareve chicken-flavored bouillon cubes or*
*6 tablespoons powdered bouillon*
*½ teaspoon salt*
*¼ teaspoon white pepper*
*½ cup mayonnaise*
*2 teaspoons dried parsley*

Place the first 7 ingredients into a 4-quart (4-liter) saucepan. Bring to a boil over high heat. Reduce the heat to low and cover. Simmer for 15 minutes or until the potatoes are tender; cool. In a blender, blend half at a time until smooth. Pour the batches into a large bowl. Stir in the mayonnaise and parsley and cover. Chill overnight.

## Gazpacho with Watermelon

And you thought you knew everything there was to know about watermelon!

Refrigerate at least 1 hour.
Makes 4 servings.

*6 cups seeded and cubed watermelon*
*1½ cups chopped Golden Delicious apples*
*½ cup finely chopped onion*
*½ cup finely chopped green pepper*
*1 teaspoon dried basil*
*½ teaspoon salt*
*¼ teaspoon coarsely ground pepper*
*¼ teaspoon chili powder*
*1 tablespoon cider vinegar*
*1 thinly sliced apple for garnish*

In a blender or food processor purée the watermelon and pour it into a large mixing bowl. Stir in the remaining ingredients and refrigerate. Serve cold. Garnish with thin apple slices. This recipe can be doubled or tripled.

DAIRY OPTION: A dollop of sour cream or yogurt can be swirled into the gazpacho.

# Main Dishes

Close your eyes and think back to the time when you were a child and couldn't wait for supper time to roll around. Perhaps there's a special aroma that brings back the memory — as well as a smile to your face and a growl to your tummy.

In the following section, I have created pareve alternatives that will elicit the same types of reactions. I think these wonderful recipes will warm your heart and stomach, as well as delight your other senses.

# Vegetarian Cholent

A terrific change of pace from the meat cholent you have every week.

Makes 8–10 servings.

*1¼ cups kidney beans*
*1 cup navy beans*
*Water*
*3 medium onions, sliced*
*1 teaspoon minced garlic*
*½ cup sliced fresh mushrooms*
*¼ cup vegetable oil*
*½ cup whole barley*
*½ teaspoon crushed dried basil or 2*
*teaspoons fresh basil*
*½ teaspoon chopped dill weed*
*Salt, pepper, paprika, cayenne to taste*
*3 large carrots, sliced*
*2 celery stalks, sliced*
*4 large potatoes, scrubbed and quartered*
*1 cup dry red wine*
*2 teaspoons soy sauce*
*1 bay leaf*
*Boiling water or vegetable stock*

If the beans have not been pre-soaked, wash them carefully, discarding any that are broken or discolored. Place them in a large saucepan and cover them with water. Bring to a boil, remove from the heat and allow then to soak for about 1 hour; then drain. In a large, heavy ovenproof pot or a crock pot set to "high," sauté the onions, garlic and mushrooms in the oil. Add the beans, barley, herbs and seasonings. Mix well. Then add the carrots, celery, potatoes, wine, soy sauce and bay leaf. Add the boiling water or stock until it's about 1 inch above all the ingredients. You can then cook this immediately on top of the stove over a medium heat, stirring occasionally, or in the oven at 350° for about the same amount of time. Simmer for about 3½–4 hours.

Or before sundown on Friday, if the ingredients are at least half-cooked, you can cover the pot tightly and allow it to simmer slowly in a 225° oven, or in a crock pot set to "low," or on a Shabbos hotplate overnight.

# Butternut Squash Stew in Bread Bowls

You can even eat the bowl!

Bake at 350° for 20–25 minutes.
Makes 4 servings.

*1 loaf frozen bread dough, thawed, divided
into fourths*
*1 egg, beaten*
*2 cups cubed butternut squash or frozen
acorn squash*
*1 tablespoon margarine*
*1 coarsely chopped onion*
*1 thinly sliced carrot*
*1 thinly sliced celery rib*
*2 teaspoons minced garlic*
*2 tablespoons chopped dried parsley*
*2 teaspoons ground cumin*
*½ teaspoon dried ginger*
*2 cups canned white kidney beans, drained*
*Salt and pepper to taste*

Roll each piece of dough into a ball. Place on a cookie sheet that has been coated with non-stick cooking spray. Brush with beaten egg. Cover with plastic wrap that has also been sprayed and let rise 2–3 hours or until doubled in size. Preheat oven. Bake until golden brown.

Meanwhile, place the squash in a steamer basket over boiling water; cover the saucepan and steam 10–12 minutes or until tender. Drain, reserving the liquid and set aside.

Melt the margarine in a heavy non-stick skillet over medium heat and add the onion, carrot, celery and garlic. Cover the skillet and cook 10 minutes, stirring occasionally, until the onion is tender. Stir in the squash

and remaining ingredients and simmer 5–10 minutes, adding enough of the reserved liquid to keep the mixture from drying out.

Let cool. To serve, cut off the top of each bread bowl, scoop out the filling and fill the bowls with the stew.

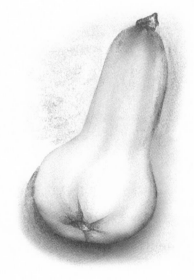

# Vegetarian Chili with Rice

On a cold, cold day this chili is guaranteed to light a fire to keep you warm. The more hot sauce you add, the warmer you get.

Simmer for about 1 hour.
Let stand for about 1 hour.
Makes 6–8 servings.

*½ cup vegetable stock*
*1 large onion, chopped*
*1 tablespoon cumin*
*1 tablespoon parsley*
*1 tablespoon garlic*
*2 tablespoons paprika*
*3 15-ounce cans pinto beans, drained*
*1 32-ounce can crushed tomatoes with juice*
*1 package onion soup mix*
*1 tablespoon hot sauce, or to taste*
*4 cups cooked rice (brown is great)*

In a large pot, sauté the onions, cumin, parsley, garlic and paprika in the vegetable stock for about 5 minutes. Then add the pinto beans, tomatoes and onion soup mix and simmer. Add the hot sauce. Add about 4 cups of cooked brown rice and let it stand. Reheat and serve or refrigerate and serve later. This tastes better if it's allowed to set awhile.

In a crock-pot, just add the sautéed onions and spices to the rest of the ingredients and let cook overnight. I add the cooked rice the next morning and leave the pot on all day. The chili usually comes out quite runny until you add the cooked rice and let it sit. The rice absorbs most of the moisture, leaving a thick, hearty chili. Less rice means a runny chili. You can make this in a crock-pot ahead of time for Shabbat.

MEAT OPTION: Sauté 1 pound ground beef, drain and add when you add the pinto beans.

# Hearty Chili

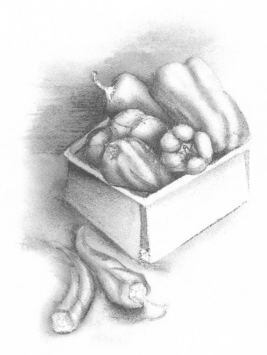

This is a stick-to-your-ribs
kind of chili;
you don't even miss the meat.

Simmer for at least 30 minutes.
Makes 6–8 servings.

*1 tablespoon olive oil*
*1 chopped onion*
*1 thinly sliced carrot*
*1 chopped green pepper*
*1 cup sliced mushrooms*
*1 small zucchini, sliced*
*12 black olives (optional)*
*4 large cloves garlic, minced*
*3 cups chopped canned tomatoes with juice*
*2 cups tomato sauce*
*½ cup diced green chili peppers*
*4 cups cooked kidney, pinto, or black beans*
*3 tablespoons chili powder*
*1 tablespoon dried oregano*
*2 teaspoons ground cumin*
*2 teaspoons paprika*
*Red pepper flakes to taste (optional)*
*Ground red pepper to taste (optional)*
*1 tablespoon white wine vinegar*
*Chopped fresh parsley to taste (optional)*

In a large stockpot, heat the oil. Add the onion, carrot, green pepper, mushrooms, zucchini, olives and garlic and sauté for about 20 minutes, stirring occasionally. Add the tomatoes (with juice), tomato sauce, chili peppers (wear plastic gloves when handling), beans, chili powder, oregano, cumin, paprika, red pepper flakes and red pepper and simmer uncovered; stir often to prevent burning. Add the vinegar and parsley and mix well. Simmer 30 minutes or more and serve.

DAIRY OPTION: Garnish with sour cream or yogurt.

MEAT OPTION: Brown 1 pound of lean ground beef, drain and add to the vegetables.

# Beef-less Stew

A hearty, full-bodied stew.

Simmer for about 30 minutes.
Makes 6–8 servings.

*2 teaspoons olive oil*
*2–3 crushed garlic cloves*
*15 small boiling onions, cut in half*
*lengthwise*
*1 pound peeled baby carrots*
*1 cup celery, cut into 1-inch chunks*
*3 medium potatoes, peeled and cut into*
*1-inch cubes*
*1 cup frozen peas*
*1 cup frozen corn*
*1 cup tomato sauce*
*¼–⅓ cup onion soup mix*
*1 cup water*
*½ cup red wine*
*1 teaspoon thyme*
*1 bay leaf*
*8 ounces extra firm frozen tofu, thawed*
*and cut into 1-inch cubes*
*½ teaspoon black pepper, freshly ground*
*3 tablespoons all-purpose flour*
*¼ cup water*

Heat oil in a large, heavy saucepan over a medium heat. Add the garlic, onions, baby carrots, celery and potatoes. Cook for 10 minutes, stirring frequently. Add the remaining ingredients EXCEPT for the flour and ¼ cup water. If necessary, add extra water so that all the ingredients are covered. Cover, reduce heat and simmer for about 30 minutes or until potatoes are tender, stirring occasionally.

In a small bowl, mix flour with the ¼ cup water until smooth. Add to the stew, stirring constantly until the liquid of the stew thickens. Remove and discard bay leaf before serving. This is great over rice or noodles.

# Crabby Cakes

Don't let the name fool you. Nothing but the sounds of everyone noisily and happily munching will greet you after you serve these. These can be served as a main dish on a bun or as a side dish. Or, you can make the patties smaller and serve them as appetizers.

Makes 6 servings.

*2 eggs*
*2 cups grated zucchini (squeeze*
*out excess juice)*
*2 tablespoons mayonnaise*
*2 tablespoons chopped onion*
*1 teaspoon seafood seasoning*
*1 cup seasoned bread crumbs*
*All-purpose flour*
*Oil or margarine for frying*

Combine all the ingredients except for the flour in a large bowl and mix well. Shape the mixture into 6 patties. Coat both sides in flour. In a skillet, heat the oil and fry patties on both sides until golden. The patties will firm up as fried.

SEAFOOD OPTION: You can add ½ cup of drained tuna to the mixture.

DAIRY OPTION: A dollop of sour cream with a little dill, salt and pepper makes a great topping.

TIP: Salt toughens eggs, so add it to egg dishes only after they are cooked.

# Spinach Rollups

"Lazy Lasagna" is probably a better name for this very easy dish.

Bake at 350° for about 25 minutes.
Makes 6–8 servings.

*2 10-ounce packages frozen spinach*
*1 tablespoon olive oil*
*2 chopped shallots or chopped slice of onion*
*2 finely chopped garlic cloves*
*1½ tablespoons margarine*
*1½ tablespoons all-purpose flour*
*1 cup non-dairy creamer*
*Pinch of nutmeg*
*½ teaspoon dried basil*
*½ teaspoon dried oregano*
*½ teaspoon dried crushed rosemary*
*2 teaspoons lemon juice (optional)*
*10–12 cooked lasagna noodles*
*2–3 cups tomato sauce*

Preheat oven. Thaw spinach and drain thoroughly. Place the spinach in a sieve and press to extract more water, but do not press so hard that the spinach goes through the sieve.

In a medium-sized saucepan, heat the olive oil and sauté shallots for 1 minute; add garlic and sauté for 1 minute more. Do not let the garlic brown. Turn down the heat to medium; add the margarine and melt. Mix in the flour and cook for about 1 minute. Slowly add the non-dairy creamer, stirring briskly all the while. Add nutmeg and herbs. Let simmer on low heat for about 10 minutes to rid the sauce of a floury taste; remove the skin that will form on top. If desired, slowly stir in the lemon juice, drop by drop. Add spinach to this sauce and stir thoroughly; the mixture should be thick.

Spoon the spinach mixture onto a lasagna noodle, leaving about half an inch unfilled at one end. Roll up from the filled end, jellyroll fashion. This may take some practice, but remember: lasagna noodles are fairly thick and forgiving.

Cover the bottom of a baking dish with tomato sauce. As the rolls are finished, stand them up in the pan so that the filling shows; leave a little space between them. When the pan is full, pour tomato sauce into the pan until the rolls are half-covered. Tightly cover the pan with foil and bake until sauce is bubbly.

OPTION: Chopped sautéed mushrooms may be added to tomato sauce.

# Asparagus Strudel

This is far easier than it sounds
and tastes twice as good
as you think it will.

Bake at 400° for 40 minutes.
Makes 4 servings.

*2 large onions, finely chopped*
*¼ cup chopped mushrooms*
*1¼ pounds plus 2 tablespoons margarine*
*1½ pounds trimmed asparagus, blanched,*
*chopped and cooked until tender*
*2 teaspoons dried dill*
*8 phyllo pastry sheets*
*1⅓ cups fine fresh bread crumbs*
*¼ cup finely chopped parsley*

**Garnish**:

*Parsley sprigs*
*Lemon slices*
*Asparagus tips*

**P**reheat oven. In a skillet, sauté the onions and mushrooms in 2 tablespoons of margarine for about 10 minutes until they are soft, but not browned. Put the onions and mushrooms in a bowl. Don't clean out the skillet. Melt about ¼ cup margarine in the skillet and add the pre-cooked asparagus. Cook slightly, stirring very well until the asparagus is coated with the melted margarine. Add the dill, mix well and remove from heat. Remove from skillet.

Melt the remaining margarine in a small saucepan. Spread one phyllo sheet out; brush it with the margarine. Put another sheet on top of the original sheet and repeat until 4 are used.

Spread half of the onion mixture evenly on top of the top phyllo sheet. Then, put half of the asparagus mixture on top of the onions and sprinkle with ⅓ of the bread crumbs and parsley. Fold over 2 inches of the phyllo dough and then roll it up like a log. Repeat with the remaining ingredients.

Place the rolls, seam-side down on a cookie sheet. Brush the top with remaining margarine and sprinkle with remaining crumbs. Bake until golden crisp. To serve, cut the logs in half and garnish with parsley, lemon and the extra asparagus tips. This can be doubled or tripled or cut into smaller pieces and served as an appetizer. Great with a yogurt or brown sauce.

# Veggie Burgers with Savory Carrots

These are not for the novice cook, but it's worth taking the time to learn.

Makes 4 servings.

### Cumin Spiced Carrots:

2 cups grated carrots
2 cups boiling water
1 tablespoon fresh lemon juice
½ teaspoon sugar
¼ teaspoon salt
¼ teaspoon cumin
¼ teaspoon paprika
Pinch of cinnamon
1 tablespoon chopped fresh parsley
2 tablespoons olive oil

### Veggie Burgers:

8 ounces white mushrooms
2 tablespoons olive oil
¼ cup diced onion
¼ cup (3–5 mushrooms) Shiitake mushrooms,
stemmed and caps diced
¼ cup finely diced red pepper
¼ cup finely diced zucchini
¼ teaspoon curry powder
¼ teaspoon cumin
1 cup cooked brown rice
1–2 eggs
¼ cup grated carrots
1 tablespoon chopped fresh parsley
½ teaspoon salt
¼ teaspoon freshly ground pepper
4 large lettuce leaves
4 crusty or whole-wheat hamburger rolls,
sliced in half
Cucumber slices for garnish

Place carrots in a colander. Pour boiling water over the carrots; drain well. In a medium-sized bowl, stir together the lemon juice, sugar, salt, cumin, paprika and cinnamon until the sugar dissolves. Stir in the carrots, parsley and oil. Makes 1¾ cups. Set aside.

Using a food processor, finely chop the white mushrooms. Heat 1 tablespoon oil in a large (10-inch) non-stick skillet over medium heat. Add the onion and cook until softened, 3–4 minutes. Add the white mushrooms and cook, stirring occasionally, 5 minutes. Add the Shiitake mushrooms, pepper, zucchini, curry powder and cumin and cook 5 minutes more, until most of the liquid is evaporated.

Meanwhile, pulse the brown rice in a food processor until finely chopped; transfer to a medium-sized bowl. Stir in the mushroom mixture, eggs (start with one egg and add another to help bind the mixture, if necessary), ¼ cup carrots, parsley, salt and pepper until well combined. Shape the mixture into four ½-inch-thick patties.

Heat the remaining 1 tablespoon oil in the same skillet over medium-high heat. Cook the patties 4–5 minutes per side until crisp and heated through. Arrange lettuce on the bottom of rolls; top each with a burger and about ½ cup cumin carrots. Cover with the top rolls. Serve with cucumbers, if desired.

# Pecan Mushroom Burgers

These are sooooo good
that you may eat the leftovers cold
right out of the refrigerator!

Broil 7–9 minutes per side.
Let stand for about 1 hour.
Makes 8–10 burgers.

*1 tablespoon olive oil*
*3 minced garlic cloves*
*1 cup chopped onions*
*½ pound sliced fresh mushrooms*
*¼ pound coarsely chopped chard leaves*
*2 teaspoons soy sauce*
*1 teaspoon rice vinegar*
*1 cup prepared bulgar*
*¼ cup pecans, toasted and ground to coarse powder*
*1¾ cups bread crumbs*
*Salt and pepper*

In a skillet, heat the oil and sauté the garlic until golden. Add onions, mushrooms, chard, soy sauce and rice vinegar. Cook over low heat, covered, until the vegetables are softened.

Place vegetable mixture and the bulgar in a food processor or blender; pulse several times until well blended. Pour the mixture into a large bowl and add the ground pecans and bread crumbs. Mix with a spoon or your hands until all the ingredients are thoroughly combined. Form into patties about a 1/2-inch thick and 3 inches in diameter.

Preheat broiler. Place patties on cookie sheet that has been sprayed with a vegetable oil spray and broil 3-5 inches from the heat until lightly browned (about 7–9 minutes). When one side is done, turn patties carefully with spatula as they can break fairly easily. Let stand for about 1 hour. (I usually serve 2 patties per person).

You can make them a little bigger and serve them as "cutlets" with a mushroom gravy if you want things a little more elegant. Great toppings include shredded lettuce or cabbage, sweet onion, tomato and cucumber.

# E-Z Bean and Rice Burrito Casserole

This is one of those throw together in fifteen minutes kind of recipes (if you have the ingredients). You can double or triple it and serve it to a house full of hungry last-minute guests and look like you spent hours in the kitchen.

Bake at 350° for 30 minutes.
Makes 6–8 servings.

*12 flour tortillas*
*3 cups canned pinto beans, rinsed and drained*
*2 cups cooked brown rice*
*½ cup finely chopped red pepper*
*1 cup chopped scallions*
*Dried parsley*

**Enchilada Sauce:**

*2 cups tomato sauce*
*3 cups water*
*¼ teaspoon garlic powder*
*½ teaspoon onion powder*
*3 tablespoons chili powder*
*4 tablespoons cornstarch*

**Toppings:**
*Chopped avocado*
*Chopped tomato*
*Chopped black olives*
*Shredded lettuce*

In a large saucepan, combine all the enchilada sauce ingredients. Cook, stirring constantly, until the mixture boils. Reduce flame and simmer while stirring, about 7–8 minutes more, until it thickens. Set the sauce aside to cool slightly.

Preheat oven. Spread 1 cup of the enchilada sauce in the bottom of a 9x13-inch casserole dish. Take one tortilla at a time and spread first beans then rice, then the red pepper and then the scallions and parsley down the center. Roll up like a log and place them seam-side-down in the casserole dish. Repeat until all ingredients are used (you may need two dishes if you don't roll them very tightly). Pour the remaining enchilada sauce over the rolled-up tortillas, cover and bake.

Remove from the oven and let cool for about 5 minutes before serving. Sprinkle on top the toppings of your choice.

MEAT OPTION: You can put cooked shredded chicken or beef on top of the beans before you add the other ingredients.

DAIRY OPTION: You can sprinkle a little Cheddar or Jack cheese over the beans before adding the other ingredients and then sprinkle a little more over the top of the casserole before baking.

# Four Grain Casserole

This casserole takes
a little bit longer to make,
but is it ever worth the effort!

Bake at 350° for 30 minutes.
Serves 4–6.

¼ cup uncooked millet
¼ cup uncooked wheat berries (available in
health food stores)
¼ cup uncooked barley
½ cup uncooked brown rice
1½ cups water
1 teaspoon olive oil
1 medium onion, coarsely chopped
2 minced garlic cloves
1 coarsely chopped celery rib
1 small red or green bell pepper, coarsely
chopped
1 coarsely chopped carrot
2 cups canned chopped tomatoes, drained
¼ cup toasted pine nuts (optional)
½ teaspoon ground nutmeg
½ teaspon ground savory
1 teaspoon curry powder
1 teaspoon dried thyme
Salt and pepper to taste

Preheat oven. Toast uncooked millet, wheat berries, barley and brown rice in a heavy pan over medium heat about 5 minutes or until nutty aroma emerges. Stir frequently while toasting. Add water. Cover and cook over low–medium heat 40 minutes or until tender.

Heat oil in a large skillet over medium-high heat. Add onion, garlic, celery, bell pepper and carrot. Sauté until onion is soft but not browned, about 5 minutes, adding water as needed to prevent scorching. Remove from heat. Add tomatoes, pine nuts, nutmeg, savory, curry, and thyme. Season with salt and pepper. Combine with cooked grains and mix well.

Spoon into lightly oiled 9x13-inch casserole or baking dish. Cover and bake.

DAIRY OPTION: Top with ⅓ cup shredded cheddar cheese before baking.

# Pueblo Corn Pie

Definitely make 2 of these,
because you'll want to keep one
all for yourself.

Bake at 375° for about 45–50
minutes.
Makes 6–8 servings.

1 tablespoon olive oil
1 large onion, chopped
2 minced garlic cloves
1 medium green or red bell pepper, diced
1½ cups fresh or thawed frozen corn
kernels, drained
2¼ cups canned or cooked pinto beans,
drained
2 cups seeded, drained and chopped ripe
tomatoes or
14- to 16-ounce can diced tomatoes,
drained well
2 teaspoons chili powder, or to taste
1 teaspoon dried oregano
½ teaspoon ground cumin
Salt to taste

**Cornmeal Topping:**
5 cups water
1¼ cups cornmeal
½ teaspoon salt

Preheat oven. Heat oil in a large skillet. Add onion and sauté until translucent; add garlic and bell pepper and continue to sauté until the onion is golden brown. Add the corn, pintos, tomatoes and seasonings; mix and simmer 10–15 minutes. Remove from the heat.

**To make the topping:**

Bring the water to a rolling boil in a heavy saucepan. Slowly pour the cornmeal in a thin, steady stream into the water, stirring to avoid lumping. Add salt and cook covered over very low heat, 20 minutes, stirring occasionally.

Grease a shallow 2-quart baking dish and line the bottom with half of the cooked cornmeal. Spoon the vegetable mixture over this and top with the remaining cornmeal mixture, spreading it smoothly. Bake until cornmeal is golden brown and crusty. Let stand 10 minutes. If the bottom is too "wet," return to the oven for an additional 5 minutes.

DAIRY OPTION: Sprinkle 1 cup of shredded Cheddar cheese over the vegetables before spreading the cornmeal on the top.

57

# Crispy Eggplant

So little time and so many people to serve? This recipe is the answer to the "What should I make tonight?" dilemma.

Makes 8 servings.

### Sauce:

⅔ cup sugar
½ cup dry sherry
3 tablespoons soy sauce
¾ cup water
2 teaspoons dried orange peel
1–2 small dried hot red peppers
sliced green onions for garnish

### Batter:

1½ cups all-purpose flour
½ cup cornstarch
½ teaspoon baking powder
Water

2 pounds eggplant
Oil for frying

### To make the sauce:

In a bowl, combine the sugar, sherry, soy sauce and water. Mix and set aside.

### To prepare the eggplant:

Wash the eggplant, but don't peel. Remove and discard the stems. Slice the eggplants crosswise into ¼-inch thick disks. (If using the longer American eggplants, cut the eggplant in half before slicing.) Set aside.

In a bowl, combine the flour, cornstarch, baking powder and enough water to make a batter the consistency of cream. Dip the eggplant slices in the batter to coat. In a large skillet or wok, heat the oil and fry the coated eggplant until golden brown. Drain the slices on paper towels.

When you've finished frying the eggplant, discard all the debris and oil from the pan EXCEPT for 1 tablespoon of the oil. Add the orange peel and dried red pepper to it and cook over a high flame for about 30 seconds. Add the prepared sauce mixture and stir constantly until the sauce thickens slightly. At this point, add the cooked eggplant and stir until all the pieces are lightly coated. Place the eggplant and sauce on a serving plate and garnish with green onions.

NOTE: The eggplant can be deep-fried to a light golden brown in advance and refried just before serving.

NOTE: This batter is great for coating vegetables when you want to make a tempura kind of dish.

### To make dried orange peel:

Use a vegetable peeler to peel the rind off an orange (try not to take off any of the white part). Put the rind on paper towels on a cookie sheet and bake at a very low temperature (below 200°) until the peel is dried. Then, break the peels into small pieces.

# Stir-Fried Eggplant with Garlic Sauce

The peppers add just the right amount of SIZZLE to make you sit up and take notice.

Stir fry about 7–8 minutes. Makes 2 main-course servings or 4 side-dish servings.

*1 cup vegetable broth*
*1 teaspoon cornstarch*
*¼ cup vegetable oil*
*1 tablespoon sesame oil*
*1 tablespoon minced garlic*
*1 large red jalapeno chili, seeded and thinly sliced*
*1 pound Japanese eggplant, cut lengthwise into quarters*
*¼ cup thinly sliced fresh basil*
*Ground white pepper and salt to taste*

Mix the broth and cornstarch in a small bowl until smooth. Heat the vegetable oil and sesame oil in a wok or heavy large skillet over a high flame. Add the garlic and jalapeno and stir until the garlic sizzles, about 10 seconds. Add eggplant and stir-fry until tender and golden, about 5 minutes. Add the basil and stir 1 minute. Stir in the broth mixture and boil until the sauce thickens and coats the eggplant, about 1 minute. Season the eggplant with white pepper and salt. Serve hot. This recipe can be doubled or tripled.

# Eggplant, Tomato Sauce and Pasta

Cook for about 15–20 minutes. Makes 6 servings.

*2 cups dry pasta shells (small shells or lasagna)*
*⅓ cup water*
*¼ cup cider vinegar*
*1 large eggplant, peeled and cubed*
*1 small red onion, chopped*
*½ cup chopped chives*
*1 tablespoon minced garlic*
*1 chopped green pepper*
*½–1 cup chopped mushrooms*
*1 medium tomato, chopped*
*10–12 ounces tomato sauce*
*3–4 tablespoons oregano*
*¼ cup red wine*
*Salt to taste*
*Ground pepper to taste*

Cook the pasta shells according to package directions. While cooking the pasta, heat the water and vinegar in a large skillet. Add the cubed eggplant, onion, chives, garlic, green pepper and mushrooms to the warm water; cook until soft, stirring often. When the vegetables are done, add to the pasta along with the tomato, tomato sauce, oregano, red wine, salt and pepper. Stir and heat gently (on low) until heated thoroughly.

DAIRY OPTION: Add ½ cup Parmesan cheese to the tomato sauce.

MEAT OPTION: Sauté 1 pound of ground beef; drain and add to the tomato sauce.

## Eggplants Stuffed with Rice

This dish will fill you up,
but not out.

Bake at 350° for about 30 minutes.
Makes 4 servings.

*1 cup cooked white rice*
*½ cup chopped onion*
*1 tablespoon pignoli (pine nuts)*
*1 plum tomato, halved, seeded and diced*
*2 teaspoons olive oil*
*2 small Italian eggplants, about*
*½ pound each*
*2 teaspoons bread crumbs*
*1 tablespoon finely chopped*
*Italian (flat leaf) parsley*
*Salt and pepper to taste*

Preheat oven. In a large bowl, combine the rice, onion, pine nuts, tomato and olive oil. Mix well and set aside. Using a spoon, carefully scoop out the eggplant flesh, leaving a ½-inch-thick shell. Chop the scooped-out eggplant very well and mix well with the rice mixture. Pack the rice/eggplant mixture into the eggplant shells. Sprinkle the top with the bread crumbs, parsley, salt and pepper. Arrange on a lightly greased baking sheet; cover lightly with foil and bake 20 minutes. Uncover and bake until tops are browned, about 10 minutes more. You can pour a warm tomato-based sauce over the top of this if you like.

DAIRY OPTION: Mix 1 teaspoon grated Parmesan cheese with the bread crumbs.

## Open-Faced Omelette

Much, much better than a regular
old cheese omlette.

Cook about 15–20 minutes.
Makes 6 servings.

*2 large potatoes, cubed small*
*1¼ cups (3–4 ears) fresh corn kernels*
*4 chopped green onions*
*2 tablespoons margarine*
*4 large eggs*
*⅓ cup non-dairy creamer*
*½ teaspoon dried basil*
*¼ teaspoon salt*
*⅛ teaspoon pepper*
*2 small tomatoes, cut into 12 wedges*

In a saucepan, cover the potatoes with water and cook until they are just soft; drain, peel and cut up. Place the potatoes, corn and green onions in a lightly greased 9-inch non-stick skillet and saute with the margarine until the onions are tender (2 minutes over a low flame), stirring constantly. Remove from heat.

In a bowl, whisk together the eggs, non-dairy creamer, basil, salt and pepper and pour over the vegetables in the skillet. Cover and cook, without stirring, over medium-low heat 10–15 minutes or until almost set. Top with tomato wedges. Cover and cook 3–5 more minutes.

DAIRY OPTION: Sprinkle ⅔ cup Cheddar cheese over the tomatoes on top of the omelette and cook as directed.

# Rice Dishes

Nowadays, rice dishes — once relegated to being served on the side — are becoming increasingly popular as main courses. Rice is both healthy and filling.

In fact, rice has always been a key nutritional component in our diet. Most rices have long been fortified with folic acid (the synthetic form of naturally occurring folate). Folic acid is a key nutrient which prevents some birth defects, and now there is evidence that folic acid may protect against heart disease and some forms of cancer.

There's such a large variety of rices available in today's marketplace that when they are combined with other folate-rich foods such as vegetables, nuts, some legumes and fruits, you can create healthy and incredibly tasty dishes that will have everyone clamoring for seconds.

## Classic Fried Rice

You can use this recipe any time you like, not just when you're serving Chinese food.

Stir-fry for 10–12 minutes.
Makes 4–6 servings.

*5 minced garlic cloves*
*1 tablespoon olive oil*
*1 diced red pepper*
*1 diced green pepper*
*2 julienned carrots*
*2 cups chopped broccoli*
*1 chopped white onion*
*2 cups frozen peas*
*2–3 cups white rice, cooked and cooled*
*4 tablespoons soy sauce*
*½ teaspoon black pepper*
*½ teaspoon garlic powder*
*2 fried eggs, shredded (optional)*

In a wok or skillet, simmer the garlic in the olive oil until it's light brown. Add the rest of the vegetables and stir-fry for approximately 5–7 minutes. Add the cooked white rice and stir-fry (stirring constantly) while adding the soy sauce. Sprinkle with black pepper and garlic powder and stir-fry for approximately 5 more minutes. Just before serving, add the fried egg and mix well.

MEAT OPTION: Add 1 cup shredded, cooked chicken or beef when you add the garlic powder.

## Unusual Couscous Pilaf

Different and delicious.

Makes 4–6 servings.

*2 cups water*
*¼ cup olive oil*
*2 cups instant couscous*
*2 tablespoons margarine (optional)*
*1 large onion, minced*
*2 medium carrots, diced*
*2 teaspoons cumin*
*1 teaspoon cinnamon*
*½ teaspoon cayenne*
*2 cups chick peas, drained*
*⅓ cup dark seedless raisins*
*⅓ cup chopped fresh parsley or mint*
*Salt to taste*

Bring water and 1 tablespoon olive oil to a rolling boil. Add couscous, cover and turn off heat. Let stand until water is absorbed, about 5 minutes. Add margarine and fluff with a fork. Heat remaining olive oil in a medium skillet and sauté the onions and carrots for 5-7 minutes. Add the cumin, cinnamon and cayenne and stir in skillet for 1 minute. Remove from heat. In a large bowl combine the carrot mixture, the couscous and the remaining ingredients. Mix well, season with salt and serve either warm or at room temperature. Recipe can be doubled or tripled.

## Italian Rice Salad

A lot of ingredients, but a REALLY simple recipe. Once you try it, plain rice will never taste the same.

Boil for 20–25 minutes.
Makes 4 servings.

*2 tablespoons olive oil*
*¾ cup rice*
*1½ cups boiling water*
*1 mashed garlic clove*
*2 mashed anchovies*
*½ teaspoon oregano*
*½ teaspoon basil*
*½ teaspoon dry mustard*
*Juice of 1 lemon*
*2 tablespoons red wine vinegar*
*⅓ cup olive oil*
*Salt and pepper to taste*
*1 medium zucchini, julienned*
*⅓ cup roasted red peppers*
*¼ cup toasted pine nuts*
*½ cup pitted black olives*

In a skillet, sauté the rice in the oil until the rice is opaque. Add the water (and salt if you like). Cover and simmer over low heat until done. Set aside to cool.

Make the dressing by combining the garlic, anchovies, herbs, dry mustard, lemon juice, vinegar and oil in a food processor. Process until smooth. Add salt and pepper to taste.

Toss a third of the dressing with the rice and then add the vegetables, pine nuts and olives. Include other vegetables if you wish (artichoke hearts, baby corn, water chestnuts, etc.). Toss with remaining dressing.

MEAT OPTION: 1 cup shredded, cooked chicken tossed in with the vegetables.

## Curried Rice Salad

Perfect for a Shabbos afternoon.
No muss, no fuss,
just pull it out of the refrigerator
and put it on the table.

Makes 6–8 servings.

*2 cups rice, cooked and cooled*
*½ finely chopped green pepper*
*½ finely chopped red pepper*
*¼ cup raisins*
*3 tablespoons dried parsley*
*2 chopped scallions*
*½ cup chopped celery*

***Dressing***:
*½ cup olive oil*
*⅓ cup white wine vinegar*
*1 tablespoon curry powder*
*1 teaspoon minced garlic*
*1 tablespoon sugar*
*Dash pepper*

Combine the completely cooled rice with remaining salad ingredients and mix well; cover and refrigerate. In a container with a cover, combine all of the ingredients for the dressing. Cover and shake well, then refrigerate. Before serving, shake the dressing again and pour it over the rice and vegetables. Mix well and serve.

## Artichoke Rice Salad

Simmer about 20 minutes.
Chill 30 minutes to 3 hours.
Makes 8 servings.

*1½ cups basmati rice*
*3 cups water*
*½ teaspoon salt*
*¼ teaspoon ground turmeric*
*2 tablespoons unsalted margarine*
*1 tablespoon fresh lemon juice*
*½ teaspoon pressed/crushed garlic*
*½ cup finely diced red onion*
*½ cup pitted black olives*
*2 teaspoons dried parsley*
*Salt and pepper to taste*
*½ cup diced ripe tomatoes*
*6 cups washed mixed salad greens*
*1 cup marinated artichoke hearts*

Wash the rice thoroughly in cool water until the water is clear; drain and set aside. In a medium saucepan, add salt and turmeric to water and bring to a boil. Add the rice and bring again to a boil. Add the margarine; reduce the heat to low, cover and simmer until the water is gone and the rice is fluffy. Remove from the heat and keep the pan covered at least 15 minutes or until completely cool. This resting period is necessary for the grains to completely absorb the moisture and retain their shape when later stirred.

Mix together the lemon juice, garlic, onion, olives, parsley, salt, pepper and tomatoes. Stir gently into the cooled rice. Chill to let the flavors mingle. When ready to serve, arrange a bed of salad greens on a serving plate. Mound the rice in the center and arrange the marinated artichoke hearts around the rice. Serve as one large salad or as individual portions.

TIP: The rice may be cooked up to one day ahead of assembling the salad.

## Rice, Avocado and Corn Salad

This looks great served in individual dishes or in a large bowl. It's hearty enough for a main course if you want something light but filling.

Refrigerate for 2 hours.
Makes 6 servings.

*2 firm-ripe avocados*
*3 cups cooked rice (brown or wild make a*
*nice change of pace)*
*1½ cups corn*
*½ cup toasted almonds*
*1 finely chopped onion*
*Assorted lettuce greens for garnish*

**Dressing:**
*1 teaspoon lemon juice*
*1 tablespoon olive oil*
*1 teaspoon rice wine vinegar*
*1 teaspoon soy sauce*

Peel and pit the avocados; chop finely. Be careful not to mash. Mix the avocado and rice together in a large bowl. Add the corn and mix well. Add the almonds and onion and again mix well. Combine all of the dressing ingredients and pour over the rice mixture. Toss gently and then refrigerate. Arrange lettuce on 6 individual salad plates and divide the salad evenly between the plates.

## Vegetable Fried Rice

A great make-ahead dish that reheats in the oven or microwave.

Makes 8 servings.

*1 tablespoon cornstarch*
*⅓ cup water*
*¼ cup soy sauce*
*3 tablespoons rice wine or dry sherry*
*½ teaspoon salt*
*6 tablespoons peanut oil*
*2 eggs, lightly beaten*
*4 cups water*
*2 finely diced carrots*
*1 teaspoon minced garlic*
*½ cup diced celery*
*1 finely diced red bell pepper*
*½ cup diagonally sliced thin zucchini*
*½ cup sliced water chestnuts*
*½ cup frozen, canned, or fresh peas*
*4 cups cold cooked rice*

In a small bowl, combine the cornstarch and water. Mix well. In a saucepan, combine the soy sauce, rice wine and salt, and heat to a simmer. Add the cornstarch mixture and cook slightly until thick; set aside.

Place a small skillet over medium heat. After a minute or so, add 2 tablespoons of the peanut oil and the eggs; stir until the eggs are firm but moist. Transfer the eggs to a small bowl and break them into small pieces. Set aside. Bring water to a boil in a small saucepan. Add the carrots and boil 1 minute; drain and rinse in cold water. Place the skillet over medium-high heat. After a minute or so, add the remaining ¼ cup of peanut oil and the garlic and stir briefly. Add the carrots, celery, red pepper, zucchini, water chestnuts and peas. Stir-fry 1 minute. Add the rice and stir-fry 1 minute more. Pour in the sauce and cook until the rice is heated through, about 5 minutes, stirring frequently. Serve hot.

MEAT OPTION: Stir in 1 cup of shredded cooked chicken with the vegetables and proceed as instructed. For a more full-bodied flavor, cook the rice in chicken stock.

## Confused Rice

Hot or cold, there's nothing confusing about how great this rice tastes.

Makes 8–10 servings.

*3 cups cooked orzo or rice*
*2 cups chopped broccoli*
*½ cup chopped celery*
*1 cup corn*
*¼ cup vegetable oil*
*1 large onion, diced*
*¾ cup diced red bell pepper*
*1 tablespoon margarine*
*3 tablespoons soy sauce*

Cook rice or orzo according to package instructions. Put the broccoli, celery and corn in a microwaveable dish and cover them with a little water. Microwave covered for 5 minutes; cool, drain and set aside. In a skillet, heat the oil and sauté the onion and red bell pepper until they are slightly soft. Add the cooked broccoli mixture and margarine and sauté 2–3 minutes more. Mix in the orzo or rice. Pour on the soy sauce and mix well. Can be served hot or cold.

# Mexican Rice

Lots of spices and plenty of flavor
will make this side dish a
top-10 favorite.

Simmer 15–17 minutes.
Makes 4–5 servings.

*1 tablespoon margarine*
*1 large onion*
*2½ teaspoons minced garlic*
*½ diced red pepper*
*½ diced green pepper*
*1¼ cups rice*
*2 cups water*
*2 teaspoons dried parsley*
*¼ teaspoon oregano*
*½ teaspoon cumin*
*¼ teaspoon cayenne pepper*
*¼ teaspoon salt*
*½ teaspoon black pepper*
*½ teaspoon Tabasco sauce*
*Dash of poultry seasoning*
*1¾ pounds peeled stewed tomatoes, cut up*
*and partially drained (crushed ones just*
*don't work)*

In a large saucepan, melt the margarine. Add the onion, garlic and peppers and cook 3–4 minutes, stirring
constantly. Add the rice and cook over
low heat till it begins to brown. Add
the water, seasonings and tomatoes.
Bring to a simmer. Cover and cook
until water is cooked out.

# Apricot and Pine Nut Pilaf

Simmer for about 30 minutes.
Makes 6 servings.

*⅓ cup pine nuts*
*¼ cup margarine*
*1 onion, chopped*
*1 cup white rice*
*1¾ cups water or vegetable broth*
*2 cup dried apricots*
*1 tablespoon dried parsley*
*2 tablespoons margarine*
*Dash pepper*

In a large saucepan, melt the margarine and brown the pine nuts. Remove the nuts but leave the
margarine in the pan. Sauté the onion
in the margarine until soft; add the
rice and sauté with the onions for 1
minute. Add the water or broth and
bring to a boil, then reduce the heat
and simmer, covered, for 20 minutes
or until most of the liquid is absorbed.
Add the apricots, parsley and reserved
pine nuts. Cook an additional 10 minutes. Toss with the remaining margarine and pepper just before serving.

# Pasta Dishes

My family could cheerfully eat pasta 3 times a week or more, calories or no calories. It's never been difficult to come up with a pasta dish that fits in with any meat or milk meal that I wanted to make (Passover notwithstanding). Pastas are great last-minute dishes and are usually easy to make.

You can avoid adding high-calorie fats by substituting other ingredients. Instead of sautéing vegetables in excessive oil, try steaming them in small amounts of water or broth, or cooking them in a non-stick skillet lightly coated with a vegetable cooking spray or just a tablespoon of olive oil. You can add flavor with lemon juice, herbs and spices.

Last but not least, be sure not to "oversauce" your pasta! The sauce should complement your pasta, not overwhelm it.

There are literally hundreds of shapes and sizes of pasta, so if one kind doesn't suit you, another one will. Just remember: From salads to kugel to main dishes, pasta is perfect.

## Spicy Lo Mein with Vegetables

You won't need a fireproof stomach for this dish. Spicy doesn't necessarily mean hot; be warned, however: it does have a bit of a kick.

Makes 6 servings.

*½ pound vermicelli noodles*
*2 teaspoons hot chili oil*
*2 teaspoons grated ginger root*
*2 minced garlic cloves*
*¼ cup thinly sliced Shiitake mushrooms*
*1 medium red bell pepper, julienned*
*2 cups chopped bok choy*
*½ cup vegetable broth*
*¾ cup sugar snap peas or snow pea pods*
*2 tablespoons Tamari or soy sauce*
*2 tablespoons seasoned or*
*regular rice vinegar*
*1 tablespoon dark-roasted sesame oil*
*¼ cup chopped peanuts or cashews*
*(optional)*

Cook noodles in boiling water until they are al dente. While they are cooking, heat the chili oil in a large deep skillet or wok. Add the ginger and garlic; cook, stirring constantly for 30 seconds. Add the mushrooms, bell pepper and bok choy and cook 3 minutes, stirring occasionally. Next, add the broth and sugar snap peas and simmer, stirring occasionally, until the vegetables are crisp-tender, 3–5 minutes. Stir in the Tamari or soy sauce and vinegar. Drain the noodles and add to the skillet with vegetables; add the sesame oil and cook 1 minute, tossing well. Sprinkle with peanuts or cashews, if desired.

## Cold Lo Mein Noodles

You'll all fight for the last noodle, so you might want to double this.

Makes 8 servings.

*2 cups (1 pound) lo mein or thin noodles*
*¼ cup sesame oil*
*2 tablespoons tahini (sesame butter)*
*½ cup tamari or soy sauce*
*4 finely chopped scallions*
*1 tablespoon grated ginger*
*dash Tabasco sauce*
*½ cup sliced cucumbers*
*½ cup sliced radishes*

Cook the noodles al dente; drain and let cool slightly. In a skillet, heat the sesame oil; add the noodles and toss for about 1 minute. Add the tahini and toss well. Let cool slightly and put the noodles in a large bowl. Add the rest of the ingredients; toss well, cover and refrigerate for at least 2 hours.

# Pad Thai

A meal in itself,
this stuff is addictive.

Makes 6–8 servings.

*1 pound angel hair pasta*
*½ cup vegetable oil*
*2 tablespoons chopped garlic*
*4 eggs, lightly beaten*
*4–6 squares fresh tofu, cubed (optional)*
*3–4 teaspoons chili powder*
*snow peas (optional)*
*¼ cup soy sauce*
*½ cup sugar*
*2 cups bean sprouts*
*8 chopped green onions*
*½ cup salted peanuts*
*2–3 quartered limes*

Cook the noodles according to the directions on the package; drain, rinse and set aside. In a large, preferably non-stick, skillet, heat half the oil over medium heat. Sauté the garlic for 1 minute; add the beaten eggs. Stir until the eggs are lightly scrambled and transfer to a small bowl for later use; transfer to a large bowl if you will be using the tofu and pea pods.

To prepare with tofu and/or pea pods, don't clean the skillet. Place the tofu into the skillet and sprinkle half the chili powder over it. Gently stir-fry until the tofu has lost some of its moisture and is coated with chili powder. If using the snow peas, add them during the last few minutes that the tofu is cooking. Add the tofu (and pea pods) to the garlic-egg mixture. If not using the tofu, add the remaining oil to the pan, heat over a low flame and add the noodles. Gently stir the noo-dles, mixing and stirring so all sides become heated. Add the (remaining) chili powder, soy sauce and sugar and stir until well mixed and until the noodles are thoroughly heated. Stir in the bean sprouts, green onions, garlic-egg-tofu mixture and peanuts and again heat thoroughly. Squeeze lime juice on top of noodles and serve with lime wedges.

This reheats very nicely; just add more fresh lime juice. It can be stored in the refrigerator for several days.

# Spinach Tomato Sauce over Rottini

This is effortless and filling
and it makes spinach taste great.
What more could you ask for?

Makes 6–8 servings.

*2 cups fresh spinach*
*¼ cup olive oil*
*3 medium shallots, minced*
*2 small carrots, diced*
*2 cups canned whole tomatoes, drained,*
*juice saved*
*1 teaspoon salt*
*¼ cup minced fresh basil*
*1 pound rottini pasta*

**B**ring salted water to a boil in a large pot for cooking the pasta. Stem the spinach and wash the leaves in a large bowl of cold water, changing the water several times until no sand appears in the bottom of the bowl. Shake the excess water from the spinach and roughly dry the leaves with paper towels. (Leaves can be damp, but not waterlogged.) Set the spinach aside.

Heat the oil in a deep pot or Dutch oven with a cover. Add the shallots and carrots and sauté over medium heat until the vegetables soften but do not brown, about 8 minutes. While the shallots and carrots are cooking, coarsely chop the tomatoes. Add the chopped tomatoes to the pot, along with ½ cup of their packing juice, the salt and basil. Use the back of a spoon to break apart the tomatoes. Simmer gently, continuing to crush the tomatoes as necessary, until the sauce thickens, about 10 minutes. Add the spinach to the pot, tossing several times to coat the leaves with tomato sauce. Cover and continue cooking, removing the lid once to stir, until the spinach has wilted, about 5 minutes. Taste for salt and adjust seasonings if necessary.

While preparing the sauce, cook and drain the pasta. Toss the hot pasta with the spinach sauce. Mix well and serve immediately.

NOTE: Prepare the sauce in a large pot, because you'll need the room for the unwilted spinach!

DAIRY OPTION: Serve with grated Parmesan cheese.

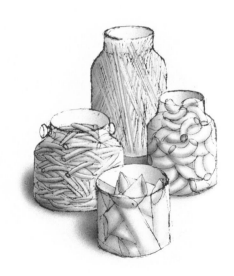

# Gingered Elbows

Forget the macaroni and cheese!
This will be the new family favorite.

Makes 6 servings.

*2 cups elbow macaroni*
*¼ cup olive oil*
*1 small onion, finely diced*
*2 minced garlic cloves*
*1 diced carrot*
*½ cup finely chopped fresh parsley*
*1 pound snap pea pods*
*1 recipe Ginger Salad Dressing*
*⅔ cup salted peanuts*

In a large pot, cook macaroni according to the package directions; rinse with cold water and drain. While the noodles are cooking, heat the olive oil in a small skillet and lightly sauté the onions, garlic, carrots, parsley and snap peas (about 2 minutes). As soon as you've drained the noodles, place them in a bowl; add the vegetables and toss. Pour the Ginger Salad Dressing over the pasta and toss gently to coat. Cover and chill for 2–8 hours. To serve, toss the salad again and sprinkle with peanuts. This recipe can be doubled or tripled. You can make it a day or two in advance. Don't, however, sprinkle the peanuts on until just before serving.

***Ginger Salad Dressing:***
*¼ cup salad oil*
*3 tablespoons rice vinegar*
*2 tablespoons sugar*
*2 tablespoons soy sauce*
*1 teaspoon grated ginger or*
*¼ teaspoon powdered ginger*
*Several dashes hot pepper sauce*

Combine all the ingredients in a jar with a lid. Cover and shake. Can be stored in the refrigerator up to 3 days.

# Southwestern Pasta

A perfect marriage
of pasta and vegetables,
with enough vegetables to make it
a main course instead of a side dish.

Let stand for at least 30 minutes.
Makes 6–8 servings.

*2 cups corn*
*2 cups penne or rottini pasta, cooked*
*2 cups chopped tomatoes*
*2 cups seeded and chopped cucumber*
*¾ cup chopped onions*
*¾ cup chopped fresh cilantro*
*2 seeded and chopped jalapeno chile peppers*
*2 cups black beans, drained*
*½ cup cider vinegar*
*3 tablespoons olive oil*
*2 teaspoons sugar*
*½ teaspoon salt*

In a large bowl, combine corn, pasta, tomatoes, cucumber, onions, cilantro, chilies, beans and vinegar. Toss and let stand at room temperature to blend flavors, or refrigerate until serving time.

Just before serving, in a small bowl, combine oil, sugar and salt. Mix well. Pour the dressing over the salad and toss gently. This can be doubled or tripled.

# Ginger Cashew Pasta Salad

A nice change from your regular pasta salads.

Refrigerate for 2–8 hours.
Makes 4 servings.

*1 cup corkscrew macaroni or fine noodles*
*20 stemmed fresh pea pods*
*1 small cucumber, quartered lengthwise and sliced*
*2 medium carrots, julienned*
*1 medium yellow and/or green sweet pepper, julienned*
*¾ cup thinly sliced radishes*
*½ cup bias-sliced green onions*
*3 tablespoons fresh cilantro*
*1 recipe Ginger Salad Dressing*
*⅓ cup chopped cashews*

Cook the pasta according to package directions; during the last 30 seconds of cooking, add the pea pods. Drain and rinse with cold water. Place the pasta and pea pods in a bowl and add the remaining vegetables. Pour the Ginger Dressing over the pasta and toss gently to coat. Cover and refrigerate. Before serving, toss salad again and sprinkle with cashews.

### Ginger Salad Dressing:
*¼ cup salad oil*
*3 tablespoons rice vinegar*
*2 tablespoons sugar*
*2 tablespoons soy sauce*
*½ teaspoon dried ginger*
*Several dashes hot pepper sauce*

Combine the ingredients in a jar with a lid. Cover and shake. Can be stored in the refrigerator up to 3 days.

# Spinach Fettuccine

The sunflower seeds and garbanzo beans lend an unexpected but nice, crunchy taste.

Preparation time: about 20 minutes.
Makes 4 servings.

*1 cup uncooked spinach fettuccine*
*1 teaspoon vegetable oil*
*1 crushed garlic clove*
*½ cup non-dairy creamer*
*2 cups shredded spinach (more if you like)*
*2 tablespoons grated lemon peel*
*½ teaspoon salt*
*2 small zucchini, thinly sliced*
*2 cups garbanzo beans, drained and rinsed*
*¼ cup toasted sunflower seeds*

Cook the fettuccine according to the directions on the package. While the noodles are cooking, in a large skillet: sauté the garlic in the oil, stir well and don't let it burn. Add the non-dairy creamer and mix well until combined and then immediately stir in the remaining ingredients, except for the noodles and sunflower seeds. Continue cooking for 2–3 minutes, stirring constantly. When the zucchini is tender, stir in the cooked noodles. Transfer to a serving dish and sprinkle with sunflower seeds to garnish. This recipe can be doubled or tripled.

# Mexican Pasta Salad

You could put this together during your siesta, it's so easy.

Refrigerate for at least 2 hours.
Makes 4 servings.

*½ pound rottini or other spiral pasta*
*2 seeded and diced tomatoes*
*1½ cups fresh corn, or frozen, thawed*
*2 shredded carrots*
*¼ cup chopped red onion*
*1 cup chopped fresh cilantro*
*Salt and pepper to taste*

**Dressing:**
*1 tablespoon Dijon mustard*
*1 tablespoon lime juice*
*1 tablespoon seeded and minced jalapeno pepper*
*¾ teaspoon chili powder*
*¾ teaspoon ground cumin*

Cook the pasta in boiling salted water 8–10 minutes or until al dente; drain and transfer to a large bowl. Add the tomatoes, corn, carrots and red onion; toss and set aside. Combine the dressing ingredients in a jar with a tight-fitting lid. Shake vigorously. Pour the dressing over the pasta, add fresh cilantro and toss thoroughly. Season to taste with salt and pepper. Cover and refrigerate. This recipe can be doubled or tripled.

OPTIONS: Try adding chopped black olives and/or celery if you like.

DAIRY OPTION: You can toss in ½ cup of shredded Cheddar cheese just before serving.

# Ruby Spaghetti

Beets are a misunderstood vegetable. They really are wonderful, but be careful: They stain EVERYTHING.

Makes 4 servings.

*⅓ cup olive oil*
*2 finely chopped garlic cloves*
*1 small onion, diced*
*Pinch of crushed red pepper, or to taste*
*2 cups finely chopped canned beets*
*1 pound thin spaghetti or linguine*
*Salt and pepper to taste*
*Fresh chopped parsley for garnish*

In a large skillet, combine the olive oil, garlic, onion and red pepper; cook over medium heat for about 30 seconds, or until the garlic is soft and the oil is sizzling. Add the chopped beets and cook, stirring constantly until heated throughout; remove from heat and set aside. Cook the pasta according to the directions on the package. Drain the spaghetti, reserving ½ cup of the cooking water. Transfer the spaghetti into the skillet with the beets. Add some of the cooking water and simmer over medium heat, constantly turning the spaghetti with the beets, until the pasta is evenly colored red, about 2 minutes. Season to taste and sprinkle on parsley for decoration. This recipe can be doubled.

# Pasta with Broccoli and Garlic

This classic Oriental dish
is still a tried-and-true, no-fail,
fallback favorite.

Makes 6–8 servings.

*1½ cups broccoli, trimmed and cut into
florets
Lightly salted water
½ cup olive oil
6 large garlic cloves, sliced paper-thin
½ cup margarine
2 teaspoons crushed red pepper flakes
1 pound rottini pasta, cooked
¼ cup sesame seeds
Cracked pepper to taste*

S team broccoli in lightly salted boiling water until it's partly done but
still crisp. Reserve 1 cup of broccoli
cooking water and drain remaining
water from the broccoli. Cut the broccoli into bite-size chunks and set
aside.

In a medium-size saucepan, heat the
olive oil over medium heat; add the
garlic slices and stir until lightly and
evenly browned. (At this point, remove and discard the garlic if you
want the taste to be subtle; if you like
garlic, then leave the slices in.) Stir in
the margarine until melted. Add the
red pepper flakes and simmer 3 minutes. Add the reserved broccoli water
and simmer another minute. Turn off
the heat and stir in the broccoli. Cover
and set aside while cooking the pasta.

Place the cooked pasta into a large
bowl and blend in the broccoli sauce.
Sprinkle with sesame seeds and black
pepper and toss to coat. This recipe
can be doubled or tripled and can be
served as a main course or side dish.

DAIRY OPTION: Serve with ¼ cup
grated Parmesan cheese.

TIP: Olive oil will keep up to two years
if stored in a tightly sealed container,
away from heat and light. During the
hot months, olive oil can be refrigerated to retain its freshness, which
may cause clouding. Clouding, however, does not affect the flavor or
quality.

# Kugels

Say the word "kugel," and instantly everyone has a mental (and emotional) response. Kugel, or kugelach, is the Yiddish word for "baked pudding" (an amusing and totally irrelevant side note is that in German, the word "kugelach" means cannonball or bullets). The traditional kugel must contain a fat (oil, butter or margarine) and eggs (or egg substitute) mixed with a starch. While there are kugels that don't contain eggs or oil, they are the exception to the rule. When describing the "best" kugel, however, family differences (and loyalties) come into play.

In my quest for the best kugel recipes, I was besieged by well-meaning friends and family begging me to try their recipes.

I assure you, the following kugel recipes are not your typical standby favorites. I tested and tasted and generally gained about 5 pounds in the hopes of finding some unique ones.

# Carrot-Apple Kugel

This kugel is wonderful enough to almost qualify as a dessert.

Bake at 350° for 20–30 minutes.
Makes 6–8 servings.

*4 cups very finely shredded (or grated) carrots*
*1½ cups finely shredded (or grated) apples*
*⅓–½ cup all-purpose flour or matzo meal*
*½ teaspoon ground nutmeg*
*1 teaspoon lemon juice*
*1 teaspoon grated lemon peel*
*½ cup toasted slivered almonds*
*¼ cup sugar to taste*
*1–2 tablespoons vegetable oil, as needed*

**Topping**:
*¼ cup toasted almonds*
*⅓ cup coconut*
*⅓ cup raisins*

Preheat oven. Lightly spray or grease a 9x9-inch baking dish. Combine all of the kugel ingredients in a bowl, using ⅓ cup of flour or matzo meal and mix until thoroughly moistened. Add more flour or matzo meal as necessary, depending on how much liquid the grated carrots and apples produce. If the mixture appears too firm, you can add 1–2 tablespoons of vegetable oil.

Depending on the type of apples you use, the kugel can vary in sweetness, from tart to overly sweet. Adjust the sugar if you wish.

Mix together the topping ingredients with a little water and spread the mixture on the top of the kugel. Bake, checking frequently. Remove from the oven when the kugel starts to turn a light golden brown.

OPTION: For a firmer kugel, use 1 cup flour and 2 eggs.

# Zucchini Kugel

Bake at 350° for about 1 hour.
Makes 6–8 servings.

*2 onions*
*5–6 medium zucchini*
*½ cup vegetable oil*
*½ cup water*
*1½ cups self-rising flour*
*1 tablespoon onion soup mix*
*3 eggs*
*Salt and pepper to taste*

Preheat oven. In a large bowl, grate the onions and zucchini together. Add the remaining ingredients and mix well. Pour into a greased 9x13-inch baking dish and bake. This freezes well and can be made in advance.

# Carrot Kugel

The raisins add extra sweetness
and the whole-wheat flour
lets you think you're really eating
something healthy.

Bake at 350° for 35 minutes.
Makes 6–8 servings.

*2 large carrots, shredded*
*½ cup vegetable oil*
*½ cup honey*
*2 eggs, separated*
*1 cup whole-wheat flour*
*½ teaspoon baking powder*
*1 teaspoon vanilla*
*1 tablespoon grated lemon rind*
*⅓ cup white raisins*
*⅓ cup chopped walnuts*

In a large bowl, combine the carrots, oil and honey. Mix well. Stir in all of the remaining ingredients except the egg whites. In a mixing bowl, beat the egg whites until stiff, but not dry; fold into the carrot mixture. Pour into a greased loaf pan and bake.

NOTE: You can double the recipe and bake it in a bundt pan, increasing baking time to 45 minutes or so. It also makes great muffins, but reduce the baking time to 20–25 minutes.

TIP: When measuring syrup or honey, first rinse the spoon or cup in cold water and the liquid won't stick to the utensil.

# Onion and Tomato Kugel

This recipe makes a lot,
so be prepared for leftovers.
The applesauce may sound like
a strange addition, but it really
lends a nice hint of sweetness
to the tomatoes.

Bake at 400° for about 1 hour.
Makes 6–8 servings.

*1 pound egg noodles*
*4 eggs*
*5 sliced plum tomatoes*
*1 large onion, sliced*
*½–1 cup unsweetened applesauce*
*1 cup vegetable oil*
*Salt and pepper to taste*
*2 teaspoons oregano*
*1 teaspoon basil*

Cook the noodles according to package directions; drain and rinse in cold water. Transfer the noodles to a large bowl and mix in all the other ingredients, adjusting the amounts of applesauce and oil to achieve the level of moistness you desire. Pour into a lightly greased 9x13-inch pan and bake uncovered until the top is golden brown.

DAIRY OPTION: Add ½ cup of Parmesan cheese when you add the herbs.

# Apple Noodle Kugel

A really sweet kugel, so
the kids will love it.

Bake at 375° for 30 minutes.
Makes 12 servings.

*1½ pounds egg noodles*
*5 peeled and cubed apples*
*1 cup raisins*
*½ cup maraschino cherries, drained and
chopped*
*1 teaspoon cinnamon*
*½ teaspoon nutmeg*
*⅓ cup orange juice*
*1 cup sugar*
*¼ cup melted margarine*
*6 eggs, slightly beaten*
*½ cup walnuts*
*1½ cups brown sugar*

Preheat oven. Cook the noodles, according to package directions, until soft, about 10 minutes; drain very well. Combine the remaining ingredients except for the brown sugar and blend well. Pour the noodle mixture into 2 greased 9x13-inch pans and bake. Remove the pans from the oven and sprinkle brown sugar over the top, trying to avoid clumps. Return the pans to the oven and bake for an additional 10 minutes. Sugar should be well-melted and the topping slightly crispy. Serve hot or cold.

# Pecan Kugel

Luscious!

Bake at 350° for 1 hour
and 15 minutes.
Makes 6–8 servings.

*¾ cup margarine*
*¾ cup dark brown sugar*
*1 cup halved pecans*
*1 pound wide noodles*
*4 large eggs*
*½ cup diced dried apricots*
*1 teaspoon cinnamon*
*1 teaspoon vanilla*
*½ cup sugar*
*2 teaspoons salt*

Preheat oven. Melt half the margarine in a 12-cup mold or 9x13-inch pan; swirl it around the bottom and up the sides. Press the brown sugar into the bottom of the pan and press the pecans into the sugar. Boil the noodles according to the package directions and drain. Transfer the noodles to a medium-large bowl. Melt the remaining margarine in a saucepan and add to the noodles. Mix in the remaining ingredients and pour into the mold. Bake until the top is brown. Let sit for 15 minutes before unmolding. The top will become slightly hard, like a praline. Serve cold or at room temperature.

# Spinach Kugel

One of the simplest kugel recipes ever created. It freezes beautifully, so you can make it in advance.

Bake at 325° for 45 minutes.
Makes 8 servings.

*2 cups (8 ounces) wide noodles*
*1½ cups cooked spinach, drained*
*1 package onion soup mix*
*½ cup sliced water chestnuts*
*1 egg*
*Chow mein noodles*

Preheat oven. Grease a 9x13-inch casserole dish and set it aside. Boil the noodles according to the package directions and drain. Mix together all of the ingredients except the chow mein noodles in a mixing bowl and then pour into the prepared dish. Cover and bake. Remove the cover and sprinkle the chow mein noodles over the top. Bake for an additional 10–15 minutes.

NOTE: If you are going to make this ahead of time, do not sprinkle the chow mein noodles over the top until you are ready to reheat it just before serving.

# Individual Vegetable Kugels

A great side dish or appetizer. You can make it as one big kugel if you're pressed for time.

Bake at 375° for 35–40 minutes.
Makes 12 servings.

*3 tablespoons margarine*
*1 medium onion, chopped*
*½ cup chopped celery*
*1½ cups grated carrots*
*¼ cup chopped red bell pepper*
*¼ cup chopped green bell pepper*
*10 ounces cooked spinach, drained*
*3 eggs, well beaten*
*¼ teaspoon ground nutmeg (optional)*
*Salt and pepper to taste*
*⅔ cup matzo meal*

Preheat oven. Grease or spray 12 muffin tins or ramekins with non-stick cooking spray. Melt the margarine in a heavy saucepan over medium-high heat. Sauté the onion, celery, carrots and peppers for 2–3 minutes, or until the onion is translucent. Set aside.

Place the drained spinach in a bowl. Add the eggs and nutmeg and mix well. Season with salt and pepper to taste. Add the sautéed vegetables and matzo meal and mix thoroughly. Spoon into the muffin tins and bake. Cool 10–15 minutes before removing from the tins. This recipe can be doubled and freezes beautifully.

# ❧ Vegetable Salads ❧

There are some mealtimes when I don't want to even contemplate turning on the oven. Then, the best solution to feeding my hungry family is a quick and easy salad.

Salads are a great way to take the fuss out of cooking. For the most part, you only need to open the refrigerator or cabinets to take out the ingredients. There is also the added bonus of the arctic breeze blowing off the crisper section when the weather is hot. I've actually stood there, happily contemplating my vegetable drawer, in the middle of a heat wave.

Salads, though, aren't just for the summer. Good, fresh produce is available all year round and the benefits of adding all that roughage and vitamins to your diet are immeasurable.

The following recipes are fast and fun. Add a loaf of bread or a roll, a piece of fruit for dessert, and you've got a meal guaranteed to get you out of the kitchen in record time.

# Great Floral Flourishes

Flowers not only look good, but taste great in salads, too! Any herb flower is edible, but you must check these flowers well for insects. Look all the way down into the piston and wash them well, too.

*Nasturtiums*: flower and leaves used in salads; peppery flavor.

*Violets*: candied and used in salads; tangy flavor.

*Lilies*: used in salads and oriental cooking; nice mellow flavor.

*Carnations/Roses*: used in salads and as garnish; rose flavor.

*Calendula*: petals used in salads; spicy like carnations.

*Dandelion leaves*: good in salads; bitter when older, so use a strong vinegar.

*Chive flowers*: good in salads; sweet onion flavor.

*Squash and pumpkin blossoms*: great stuffed and fried; tastes like squash.

*Pansies*: the whole flower is great in salads.

## Freezer Slaw

This may sound like an unusual
way to make slaw,
but the farmer's wife who
gave me this recipe loves it.

Freeze for 3 hours and then
refrigerate for several hours.
Makes 4–6 servings.

*1 head cabbage*
*1 teaspoon salt*
*1 cup white vinegar*
*½ cup water*
*2 cups sugar*
*1 teaspoon mustard seed*
*1 teaspoon celery seed*

Shred the cabbage. Sprinkle the salt on the cabbage. Allow to stand for 1 hour and squeeze dry. In a large stockpot, combine the cabbage with the rest of the ingredients. Mix well and bring to a boil, allowing to boil for 1 minute. Pour the mixture into a freezer-safe glass bowl and place in the freezer for 1 hour.

Remove from the freezer and let sit in the refrigerator to set. This recipe can be doubled or tripled. You can add red or green peppers, celery and/or shredded carrots to taste just before freezing, if desired.

## Red Cabbage Slaw

Red cabbage is a change of pace
from the green variety we
usually use and the pineapple juice
and raisins add a nice touch.

Makes 6–8 servings.

*2 cups shredded red cabbage*
*⅓ cup thinly sliced red bell pepper*
*⅓ cup thinly sliced yellow bell pepper*
*¼ cup raisins*
*2 tablespoons virgin olive oil*
*¼ cup mayonnaise*
*2 tablespoons pineapple juice*
*2 dashes Tabasco sauce (optional)*
*Salt and freshly cracked black pepper to taste*

In a large bowl, combine the cabbage, peppers and raisins. In a small bowl, combine the remaining ingredients and whisk together well. Pour the dressing over the cole slaw and toss well. You can double, triple or even quadruple this recipe.

## Broccoli Slaw

This salad is wonderful
with deli or smoked fish.

Makes 5 servings.

### *Dressing*:
*⅓ cup light mayonnaise*
*2 teaspoons vinegar*
*1 teaspoon non-dairy creamer*
*1 teaspoon sugar*
*¼ teaspoon salt*

*1½ cups cooked and shredded broccoli
stems*
*1 cup shredded carrot*
*¼ cup chopped red or white onion*
*¼ cup chopped fresh parsley (optional)*

Combine all of the dressing ingredients in a large bowl. Add the remaining ingredients. Toss to mix and
coat.

NOTE: Shred the broccoli stems and
the carrots in a food processor fitted
with a shredding disk, or use the large
holes of a 4-sided grater.

TIP: Mustard added to a salad dressing
will hold together the oil and vinegar.

## Apple Cole Slaw

This slaw is perfect for a Fall meal
when the apples are fresh.

Makes 4–6 servings.

*4 cups shredded cabbage*
*3 coarsely shredded Washington or Granny
Smith apples*
*2 coarsely chopped kiwis*
*2 bias-sliced green onions*
*Mixed salad greens for garnish*
*1–2 sliced apples for garnish*

In a large bowl, combine the cabbage, apples, kiwis and green onions. Toss with Honey Lime Dressing.
Line individual salad plate with lettuce. Arrange the apple slices on the
lettuce. Spoon the salad over the sliced
apples. This recipe can be doubled or
tripled.

### *Honey Lime Dressing*:
*⅓ cup honey*
*¼ cup lime juice*
*½ teaspoon salt*
*½ teaspoon pepper*

In a small bowl, combine all the ingredients. Mix well and pour over salad.

# Cabbage and Apple Salad

—⚬—

This recipe is fool-proof.
Even my husband, who *never* cooks,
can successfully prepare this.

**Makes 6 servings.**

*1 pound shredded cabbage*
*2 peeled and shredded Jonathan or*
*Mackintosh apples*
*2 shredded carrots*
*⅓ cup store-bought poppyseed dressing*
*¼ cup chopped walnuts*

In a large bowl, combine the cabbage, apples and carrots. Pour the dressing over the cabbage and toss. Sprinkle with walnuts and serve. This can be made in large quantities.

TIP: Be careful that you don't use too much dressing when doubling this recipe. Sometimes it's best to add only half the dressing at first and then add as needed.

# Cole Slaw Soufflé

—⚬—

This wiggles and jiggles and is a great start to any meal.

Refrigerate/freeze about 4 hours.
Makes 10–12 servings.

*1 cup crushed pineapple (do not use fresh)*
*1 3-ounce package kosher orange gelatin*
*¾ cup boiling water*
*¾ cup mayonnaise*
*1 cup shredded cabbage*
*1 cup shredded carrots*
*½ cup raisins*
*½ cup chopped walnuts*
*3 egg whites*

Drain the pineapple (reserve liquid). In a medium-size bowl, dissolve the gelatin in the water and add the pineapple liquid; mix well until the gelatin is completely dissolved. Beat in the mayonnaise, making sure that there are no lumps. Pour the gelatin into a loaf pan and place in the freezer until slightly firm to the touch about 1 inch from the edge (about 20 minutes). Remove from the freezer and place the mixture in a large bowl; beat until fluffy and then fold in the remaining ingredients, except the egg whites. Beat egg whites until stiff. Next, fold in the egg whites and set aside for a moment.

Make a collar around a 1-quart soufflé dish by folding a 22-inch piece of tinfoil in half lengthwise and taping it around the edge of the dish. Lightly oil the dish and then pour in the gelatin mixture. Chill until set. This recipe can be tripled.

# Red Cabbage and Pepper Salad

— ✦ —

Refrigerate for at least 30 minutes
but no more than 4 hours.
Makes 6–8 servings.

*½ head grated or sliced red cabbage*
*1 head shredded iceberg lettuce*
*6–8 thinly sliced green onions*
*1 diced red pepper*
*¼ cup toasted sesame seeds*
*½ cup toasted sliced almonds*

### Dressing:

*½ cup sugar*
*½ cup vinegar*
*⅓ cup oil*
*1 teaspoon salt*

In a jar with a lid, combine the ingredients for the dressing. Cover and shake well and set aside. In a large bowl, combine the ingredients for the salad and toss. Drizzle the dressing over the top, toss and chill.

NOTE: I keep the grated cabbage and sliced onion ready in resealable plastic bags. I also prepare the dressing ahead of time and then just toss everything together the day I plan on serving it. If you put it together too early, the cabbage bleeds into the dressing and gets too soggy.

# Sweet and Sour Cauliflower Salad

— ✦ —

This is a hearty salad that could be a main course if you're looking for something to pair up with a bowl of soup or a sandwich.

Refrigerate for at least 3 hours.
Makes 6 servings.

*1½ pounds cauliflower*
*1 cup pineapple chunks in juice*
*1 teaspoon cornstarch*
*1 teaspoon brown sugar*
*2 tablespoons malt vinegar*
*1 tablespoon soy sauce*
*1 tablespoon water*
*1 tablespoon tomato paste*
*2 teaspoons sherry*
*1 cup sliced water chestnuts, drained*
*3 cups shredded iceberg lettuce*

Divide the cauliflower into small florets, wash, drain and set aside. Drain the pineapple and save the juice. In a large pot of salted boiling water, cook the cauliflower for 4 minutes. Remove from heat, drain well and set aside.

In a large saucepan, combine the cornstarch, brown sugar, vinegar, soy sauce, water, tomato paste and sherry. Mix well. Add the water chestnuts, pineapple chunks and juice. Bring the mixture to a boil and simmer for 3 minutes.

Place the cauliflower in a large bowl. Pour dressing over the cauliflower. Mix well and cover. Refrigerate. Just before serving, add the lettuce and toss.

# Asparagus and Egg Salad

—✌—

When the other kids
in my son's kindergarten class
were asked what their favorite
vegetable was, they named carrots,
peas and other common vegetables.
Mine, on the other hand,
said that asparagus was his favorite,
but only with a light vinaigrette!

Makes 6 servings.

½ cup chopped dill pickles
2 coarsely chopped hard–boiled eggs
1 cup chopped mushrooms
2 cups fresh asparagus spears, cooked but
still crispy and cut into thirds
½ cup mayonnaise
1 teaspoon lemon juice
3 tablespoons vinegar
⅓ cup white wine
Salt to taste
Dash of sugar
3 minced garlic cloves

Place the pickles, eggs, mushrooms and asparagus into a bowl and set aside. In another bowl, mix together the mayonnaise, lemon juice, vinegar and wine. Add the salt, sugar and garlic to the mayonnaise mixture and mix well; adjust the spices according to taste. Pour the dressing over the salad and mix well. Serve over salad greens. This recipe can be doubled or tripled. Don't make it more than 3 hours ahead of serving, as the asparagus will become soggy.

TIP: The greener leaves on the outside of a head of lettuce contain more vitamins than the inside leaves, so try not to discard them.

# Carrot Salad with Green Onions

—✌—

Having tried to grow carrots
for 3 years in a row
only to have the rabbits devour them
just days before they were ready
to be picked has cured me forever
of wanting to garden.
Now I buy all the carrots I need
for this salad.

Refrigerate at least 2 hours but no
more than 7 hours. Let stand for an
additional hour before serving.
Makes 8 servings.

2 pounds coarsely grated carrots
6 chopped green onions
3 tablespoons minced fresh parsley
3 tablespoons white wine vinegar
1 tablespoon grated lemon peel
2 teaspoons Dijon mustard
½ cup olive oil
Salt and pepper to taste
8 whole red cabbage leaves

Mix the carrots, green onions and parsley together in a large bowl; set aside. Next, whisk the vinegar, lemon peel and mustard in a small bowl. Gradually whisk in the oil. Season the dressing to taste with salt and pepper. Pour the dressing over the carrot mixture. Toss, making sure the carrots are well coated. Cover and refrigerate.

Let stand at room temperature before serving. Spoon the salad onto cabbage leaves; arrange on a platter or individual serving plates and serve.

# Cranberry Salad

This is the perfect combination of sweet, tangy and crunchy.

Refrigerate for 2 hours.
Makes 8 servings.

¾ cup dried cranberries
1 cup semi-dry red wine
¼ cup fresh-squeezed lime juice
2 teaspoons Dijon mustard
¾ teaspoon salt
1 cup olive oil
3 Granny Smith apples
1 pound walnuts (pieces are fine)
¼ cup thinly sliced scallions
2 bunches watercress
1 tablespoon freshly grated lime zest

Place the cranberries in a bowl and cover them with the wine. Let stand at room temperature for 1–2 hours.

In a large glass bowl, combine the lime juice, mustard and salt. Mix well. Mix further while adding the olive oil in a slow stream, mixing until all the ingredients are well combined. Core and cut the apples into bite-size chunks and place in a bowl. Add the walnuts and scallions and mix well. Pour the dressing over the apple mixture and cover. Marinate in the refrigerator.

Remove the coarse stems from the watercress. Line a glass bowl or platter with the cleaned watercress. Arrange the apple mixture around the edge of the platter or bowl; drain the cranberries and spoon into the center of the dish. Sprinkle the salad with lime zest and serve immediately.

# Raspberry Spinach Salad

This elegant salad is perfect for a luncheon with the sisterhood, or when the in-laws are coming over.

Makes 6–8 servings.

2 tablespoons raspberry vinegar
2 tablespoons red raspberry preserves
1 tablespoon plus 1 teaspoon olive oil
2 tablespoons plus 2 teaspoons water
2 pounds stemmed spinach leaves, torn into pieces
¼ cup pecan halves, toasted if desired
2 cups red raspberries
2 quartered and sliced kiwis
¼ cup alfalfa sprouts

In a jar with a tight-fitting lid, combine the vinegar, preserves, oil and water. Shake vigorously until well combined; set aside.

In a large salad bowl, combine the spinach, half the pecans and half the raspberries. Toss the dressing with the salad and then sprinkle the top with the kiwi slices, remaining pecans, sprouts and remaining raspberries.

TIP: Spinach cleans faster in warm water.

# Vegetable Dishes

**M**ention of the word "vegetables" in my house sends everyone running for cover. Unless they're disguised in a sauce or hiding under a noodle, they just don't stand a chance.

I've learned to become a little devious (and I understand I'm in good company): I've learned to sneak in a mushroom here and a lima bean there. My gourmet eaters are clueless to the fact that they're consuming foods that are actually good for them.

We haven't given up junk food and high-calorie snacks entirely in our house, but we have started to enjoy a much healthier eating style. There may be hope for us yet!

# Garden Harvest Jambalaya

Perfect when the Fall vegetables are abundant and you're looking for something special for the holiday meals.

Makes 8 servings.

*1 tablespoon olive oil*
*1 large onion, diced*
*3 minced garlic cloves*
*2 seeded firm-ripe tomatoes, 1 chopped and 1 sliced*
*1 coarsely chopped red pepper*
*4 largely cubed kohlrabi*
*2 carrots, halved lengthwise, then cut into 2-inch pieces*
*½ teaspoon cayenne pepper (optional)*
*½ teaspoon black pepper*
*1⅓ cups long-grain white rice*
*2¼ cups vegetable broth*
*1 zucchini, quartered lengthwise, then cut into 2-inch pieces*
*1 cup green beans, cut into 2-inch pieces*
*Salt and pepper to taste*

In a 6- to 8-quart pan over medium heat, sauté the onion and garlic in the oil, stirring occasionally until the onion is limp, about 4 minutes. Stir in the chopped tomato, bell pepper, kohlrabi, carrots, cayenne and black pepper. Cover and simmer, stirring occasionally, until the kohlrabi is barely tender, 7–8 minutes. Stir in the rice and broth and bring the mixture to a boil over high heat; cover and reduce the heat to simmer about 20 minutes. Add the zucchini and green beans and continue simmering, covered, until the beans are just tender when pierced, about 10 minutes. Add salt and pepper to taste. Spoon onto a serving dish and top with sliced tomato.

MEAT OPTION: Brown 2 boneless, skinless chicken breasts, cut into small pieces, in the oil, onion and garlic and then cook as directed.

# Brussels Sprouts in Beer

Not for the faint of heart, but delicious.

Simmer for 20 minutes.
Makes 4 servings.

*1 pound fresh Brussels sprouts*
*Beer (enough to cover sprouts)*
*½ teaspoon salt*
*Freshly ground black pepper to taste*
*2 tablespoons margarine*

Trim and wash the Brussels sprouts. Place them in a medium-size saucepan and pour enough beer over the Brussels sprouts to cover. Bring the beer to a boil, reduce the heat and simmer until tender; add more beer to complete the cooking process, if the liquid evaporates. Drain; add salt, pepper and margarine. Serve hot. This recipe can be doubled.

## Red Pepper Latkes

Who said latkes were just for
Chanukah?

Makes 12 latkes.

2 roasted bell peppers
½ cup fresh or frozen corn kernels
1 finely chopped shallot
1 tablespoon olive oil
2 tablespoons margarine
Salt and freshly ground black pepper to
taste
1 cup pareve sour cream
1½ cups flour
1 tablespoon baking powder
1 teaspoon salt
1 cup non-dairy creamer
3 eggs, separated
2 tablespoons minced chives for garnish
8 sprigs cilantro, leaves only, for garnish

Dice 1 bell pepper. Cut remaining bell pepper in half. Cut 1 half into very thin strips. Mince the other half to consistency of purée and set aside.

Sauté corn, diced bell pepper, bell pepper strips and shallot in 1 tablespoon olive oil and margarine for 2 minutes. Season the mixture with salt and pepper to taste and stir in the pareve sour cream. Simmer over medium-low heat 10 minutes. Set aside to cool.

Sift flour, baking powder and 1 teaspoon salt together into bowl. Stir in the non-dairy creamer and egg yolks. Set the mixture aside.

In another bowl beat the egg whites until they form soft peaks, then fold them into the egg yolk mixture. Fold in the minced peppers.

Lightly brush a skillet with olive oil and heat it over a medium heat until a drop of water sizzles when dropped in. Spoon or pour 3-inch wide latkes into skillet and fry over medium heat, 2–3 minutes per side.

To serve, place warm pepper-and-corn sauce on each plate and top with 2 latkes. Garnish with chives and cilantro.

## Tomato Barley Casserole

Bake at 325° for 80–90 minutes.
Makes 6 servings.

1 cup tomato sauce
1 cup vegetable stock
1 cup white wine (can substitute more stock
for wine)
1 cup pearl barley
2 cups diced vegetables (carrots, onions,
celery and roasted red pepper)
1 medium-size ripe tomato, diced
¼ teaspoon cumin
1 teaspoon Italian herb seasoning
¼ teaspoon paprika

Preheat oven. In a 3-quart casserole dish, mix all the ingredients together and cover. Bake. Remove the cover and increase the temperature to 350°; bake until the liquid is absorbed and the top is crunchy. Do not double this recipe.

## Carrot Puffs in Sweet Sauce

This is truly an elegant vegetable dish that will disappear in no time. You can make it ahead and have time to relax before dinner.

Makes 4–5 servings.

### Puffs:

2 cups finely grated carrots
2 cups all-purpose flour
2 eggs, well beaten
⅓ cup orange juice
1 teaspoon cinnamon
½ teaspoon salt
½ teaspoon grated orange rind
2 tablespoons margarine

### Sauce:

1 tablespoon cornstarch
⅓ cup water
⅓ cup orange juice
½ cup raisins
⅓ cup currant jelly
¼ cup diced dried apricots
½ teaspoon grated orange rind

In a food processor, combine the carrots, flour, eggs, orange juice, cinnamon, salt and grated orange rind. Mix until it's combined but not puréed; it will be thick. Shape the mixture with your hands into 8–10 patties. Melt the margarine in a large skillet over medium heat. Add the patties and sauté until golden on each side and cooked through. Keep warm. These can be made ahead of time and reheated just before serving.

In a saucepan, combine the cornstarch with the water. Stir in the orange juice, raisins, currant jelly, apricots and grated orange rind. Cook over medium heat, stirring frequently until the mixture thickens and boils. Spoon the sauce over the puffs before serving. Serve warm.

NOTE: If you want to cut down on fat you can bake (350°) the puffs on a greased baking sheet for 10–15 minutes, until golden on each side and cooked through. Form the mixture into thicker patties, paying attention that they don't dry out when baking.

## Beans and Corn Sauté

Makes 4 servings.

1 tablespoon olive oil
1 medium onion, diced
2 cups cooked lima beans
2 cups fresh string beans, steamed
1 cup chopped, seeded tomatoes
½ cup whole kernel corn
½ teaspoon paprika
Dash cayenne pepper
½ teaspoon salt (optional)

In a large skillet, heat the oil and sauté the onion until golden brown. Add the other ingredients and toss well until thoroughly heated, about 5 minutes. Remove from the heat and serve immediately. You can double or triple this recipe.

## Sweet Potatoes and Apples

This will become a year-round favorite for anyone who loves sweet potatoes. The cherries add a beautiful red glaze and just the right amount of tang.

Makes 8–10 servings.

*4 pounds sweet potatoes, peeled and cut into ¼-inch slices*
*4 pounds peeled and sliced Jonathan apples*
*2 cups apple cider*
*1⅓ cups dried cranberries or dried cherries*

Place the potatoes in a steamer basket over boiling water. Cover the pan and steam 10 minutes or until tender. Remove from the heat and set the potatoes aside to cool.

Place the apples, cider and cranberries in another saucepan over medium heat; cover and cook for about 5 minutes, or until the apples soften. When the apples are cooked, drain the mixture and add the sweet potatoes. Continue cooking over low heat, stirring constantly several minutes until warm throughout. Serve immediately.

NOTE: Don't let the potatoes get too soft, or they will turn into mush.

## Orange Asparagus Bundles

This is a knock-'em-over kind of side dish and takes only minutes to prepare.

Makes 12 servings.

*3½ pounds trimmed asparagus*
*4 oranges, peels only*
*½ cup orange juice*
*¼ cup white wine vinegar*
*¾ cup olive oil*
*1 tablespoon honey*
*½ teaspoon salt*
*¼ teaspoon pepper*
*Pine nuts, as desired*

In a large skillet over high heat, bring 1 inch of salted water to a boil. Add half of the asparagus and cook 5 minutes or until tender. Using a slotted spoon or tongs, transfer the asparagus to a bowl of ice water. Repeat with the remaining asparagus. Drain and divide the asparagus into 12 bundles. With a vegetable peeler, remove a 1x7-inch strip of orange peel from each orange. Cut each strip into four ¼ inch-wide strips. Repeat with the remaining oranges to make a total of 12 strips. Tie each bundle with the orange strips. Place the bundles on a serving platter. In a medium-size bowl, combine the remaining ingredients, except the pine nuts and whisk together. Spoon the dressing over the bundles and sprinkle the pine nuts over them. This can be served at room temperature or warmed in the microwave for about 30 seconds.

# Artichoke and Spinach Mix-Up

This is a knock-off of a classic dairy dish. Quite frankly, this is better.

Bake at 350° for 30–40 minutes.
Makes 8–10 servings.

*2 cups artichoke hearts, drained*
*2 pounds chopped cooked spinach, drained*
*1 cup mayonnaise*
*½ cup margarine*
*2 tablespoons dried minced onion (or sautéed fresh)*
*Dash or two Worcestershire sauce*
*½ cup bread crumbs*

Preheat oven. Grease a 2-quart casserole dish with vegetable cooking spray (or a 9x13x2-inch baking pan, but I prefer the deeper dish). Slice the artichoke hearts onto the bottom of the dish. Combine all the other ingredients, except the bread crumbs and spoon onto the artichoke hearts. Sprinkle the bread crumbs on top and bake. Remove from the oven and let rest for 5–10 minutes before serving.

DAIRY OPTION: Substitute cream cheese for mayonnaise and butter for margarine. Low-fat or non-fat cream cheese works, too. You can also add a little more onion and Worcestershire sauce for more kick.

# Broccoli with Walnuts and Raisins

3 of the 5 food groups all in one dish.

Cook for about 10 minutes.
Makes 4 servings.

*¼ cup olive oil*
*3 minced garlic cloves*
*½ cup chopped onion*
*¼ cup chopped walnuts*
*1 bunch broccoli, trimmed and cut into florets*
*¼ cup dry white wine*
*¼ cup blanched raisins, drained*
*Salt and freshly ground pepper to taste*

In a large skillet, heat the oil and sauté the garlic, onion and walnuts, until the onion is soft. Add the broccoli, wine and raisins and season with salt and pepper. Mix well, cover and cook over low heat until the broccoli is tender. This recipe can be doubled or tripled.

MEAT OPTION: You can cook a package of Kosher Beef Fry and crumble it in just before serving.

# Chili Potato Pancakes

Hot, hot, hot
is what you get with these
scrumptious pancakes.

Makes 20–24 pancakes.

*3 peeled potatoes*
*3 large eggs, beaten*
*¼ cup chopped green chilies, drained*
*1 cup corn, drained*
*⅓ cup chopped green onions*
*¼ cup all-purpose flour*
*1 envelope onion soup mix*
*3–5 tablespoons olive oil*

In a large bowl, coarsely grate the potatoes. Let them sit for several minutes, then drain on several layers of paper towels until almost dry. Return the grated potatoes to the bowl and add the eggs, chilies, corn, green onions, flour and onion soup mix. Mix well and let set for 3–4 minutes.

In non-stick skillet, heat 2 tablespoons oil over medium-high heat. Drop a large tablespoonful of the potato mixture onto the skillet. Cook on each side until golden brown, pressing down lightly with the spatula when turning; drain on paper towels. Repeat with the remaining potato mixture, adding oil as needed. Serve with applesauce.

# Corn and Zucchini Fritters

These are better than bread
and will disappear
as fast as you can make them.

Serves 6–8.

*1½ cups corn kernels*
*½ small red onion, thinly sliced*
*1 cup loosely packed parsley sprigs*
*3 small zucchini, julienned ¾-inch*
*½ cup all-purpose flour*
*½ teaspoon salt*
*¼ teaspoon freshly ground black pepper*
*3 tablespoons club soda water*
*Vegetable oil for deep frying*

In a large bowl, combine the corn, onion, parsley and zucchini and toss to mix. Add the flour and toss with your hands, separating all the ingredients to be sure they are coated evenly with the flour. Add the salt, pepper and soda water and mix all together. The mixture should be airy and light, but not wet; do not over mix.

In a large saucepan or deep fryer, heat about 4 inches of vegetable oil to 375°. Gather the batter into loose, very free-form fritters about 3 inches in diameter. Fry 2 at a time, until they are golden brown, about 3–4 minutes, turning over halfway through. Remove with either a slotted spoon or tongs and drain on paper towels, keeping warm in an oven set to low.

# Apricots and Potatoes

Yes, this is an odd combination,
but it tastes great.

Bake at 350° for 40–50 minutes.
Makes 4 servings.

*4 medium potatoes, scrubbed and finely
sliced*
*½ cup chopped dried apricots*
*3 chopped green onions*
*½ cup water*
*2 tablespoons sweet chili sauce*
*1 tablespoon balsamic vinegar*
*1 tablespoon margarine*
*Lots of ground black pepper*

**P**reheat oven. Lightly grease an oven-proof baking dish; arrange the potato slices in layers across the bottom. Sprinkle the apricots and onions over the potatoes and cover with the remaining potato slices. Mix together the water, chili sauce and vinegar and pour over the potatoes. Dot with margarine and add the black pepper. Cover and bake until the potatoes are tender. Uncover and grill until golden. This recipe can be doubled.

# Salsas, Savory Sauces, Gravies & Salad Dressings

I used to be a ketchup kind of gal, always drowning my fries in it and slathering it on sandwiches. For years, that bottle of red "gold" was a part of almost every table I set and seemed to be part of an amazing amount of favorite dishes. I finally have to admit, though, that something has replaced it in my culinary affections.

My new love is salsa. Some recent public surveys also show that salsa has replaced ketchup as the no. 1 condiment. Salsa recipes are springing up everywhere. It's not just about tomatoes anymore: Everything from bananas to strawberries is allowed. I've used it as a marinade, a salad dressing, a dip and as an appetizer. The best thing about salsa is that it is pareve, so it can go with just about anything.

Just a quick note: If for some reason the salsa you make is too "hot," don't use water to cut the burning sensation in your mouth. Water will only spread the heat. Eat a dairy product (e.g., milk, sour cream, butter) or a piece of bread or cracker to ease it.

## Salsa in Tortilla Cups

An outstanding start to any meal, or just a fun salsa to eat with chips.

Bake at 400° for 6 minutes.
Makes 35 servings.

*10 tortillas*
*Vegetable oil*

**Dressing**:
*1 tablespoon dark rum or tequila*
*1½ teaspoons Dijon mustard*
*1½ teaspoons red wine vinegar*
*1½ teaspoons grated orange rind*
*1 tablespoon orange juice*
*¼ cup vegetable oil*

**Salsa**:
*1 pound cooked black beans, drained*
*2–3 seeded, minced jalapeno peppers*
*1 tablespoon chopped green onions*
*1 chopped navel orange*
*2 tablespoons finely chopped red pepper*

Preheat oven. Cut the tortillas into 2- to 3- inch rounds. Brush with oil on both sides; press into miniature muffin pans and make a small cup out of it. Bake until crisp. Remove from the oven and set aside to cool.

In a medium-size bowl, whisk together all the dressing ingredients. Then add all the salsa ingredients. Mix well. Fill each cup with a spoonful of salsa.

OPTION: Skip the tortilla cups and go right for the salsa.

## Traditional Salsa

Refrigerate for at least 2 hours.
Makes 3–4 cups.

*4 large tomatoes, finely chopped*
*3 Roma tomatoes, finely chopped*
*1 medium onion, finely chopped*
*3 chopped green onions*
*½ chopped green pepper*
*1 finely chopped, seeded green jalapeno pepper (optional)*
*2 finely chopped yellow chilies*
*1 teaspoon minced garlic*
*3 tablespoons chopped fresh cilantro*
*4 drops hot pepper sauce*
*2 tablespoons red wine vinegar*
*Salt to taste*

In a large bowl, combine all the ingredients and mix well. Refrigerate. You can chop the ingredients in a food processor or blender for a smoother consistency. Add more jalapenos for an increased kick.

## Salsa Verde

Translated, this means "green salsa."

Simmer for about 5 minutes.
Makes 1½ cups.

*2 tablespoons vegetable oil*
*½ cup sliced green onions*
*¼ cup fresh chopped cilantro or parsley*
*1–2 seeded jalapeno peppers*
*1 clove garlic*
*¼ teaspoon salt*
*1½–2 cups tomatillos (green tomatoes with*
*a brown papery covering)*

In a blender or food processor, combine everything except the tomatillos. Blend till smooth. Add tomatillos, ½ cup at a time. Blend for about 30 seconds after each addition (may still be a little chunky). Place the mixture in a saucepan and bring to a boil, stirring frequently. After the mixture has boiled, reduce the heat and simmer, uncovered, until it slightly thickens. Remove from the heat; cover and chill. May be refrigerated in a tightly covered container for 2–3 weeks.

## Banana Salsa

The bananas need to be firm but not green for this salsa to come out right.
This is great with grilled fish.

Refrigerate for at least 2 hours.
Makes 2 cups.

*½ cup diced red bell pepper*
*½ cup diced green bell pepper*
*1 seeded and minced jalapeno pepper*
*1 tablespoon minced fresh ginger*
*3 finely chopped green onions*
*¼ cup chopped cilantro leaves*
*¼ teaspoon ground cardamom*
*1 tablespoon olive oil*
*2 large bananas, diced*
*Salt and freshly ground pepper to taste*
*3 tablespoons fresh lime juice*
*2 tablespoons packed light brown sugar*

Combine all of the ingredients in a mixing bowl and gently toss to mix. Cut the bananas last to prevent browning. Adjust the seasonings, adding salt, pepper, lime juice and/or sugar to taste. Cover and refrigerate.

## Melon Salsa

This salsa is best when made in the summer with the freshest of the fresh melons.

Refrigerate for at least 3 hours.
Makes 6–8 servings.

*¼ cup olive oil*
*1 teaspoon minced garlic*
*1 small red onion, finely chopped*
*¼ cup lime juice*
*½ teaspoon salt*
*2 large cucumbers, seeded and diced*
*1 diced seedless orange*
*1 diced mango*
*1 diced tart apple*
*1 cup diced watermelon*
*1 cup diced cantaloupe*
*1 medium jicama, chopped*
*½ diced green bell pepper*
*1 tablespoon chili powder*

In a small bowl, combine the olive oil, garlic, onion, lime juice and salt. Mix well and let stand for 20 minutes. Place all of the cut-up fruit and vegetables in a large salad bowl; sprinkle with the chili powder and toss gently. Add the olive oil/lime juice mixture and toss to combine thoroughly. Refrigerate.

## Strawberry Salsa

This is great with chicken or fish, or served on greens as a salad dish.

Refrigerate for at least 2 hours.
Makes 2–2½ cups.

*½ red onion, diced*
*½ red bell pepper, diced*
*½ yellow bell pepper, diced*
*½ green pepper, julienne*
*¼ cup fresh minced parsley*
*1½ cups fresh sliced strawberries*
*¼ cup orange juice*
*2 tablespoons lime juice*
*2 tablespoons olive oil*
*Salt and pepper to taste*

Place all the ingredients in a large mixing bowl and toss to combine. Cover and refrigerate. Don't make it too far in advance, as the strawberries can get mushy.

OPTION: You can use blueberries or raspberries instead of strawberries, if you like, or all three.

## Mock Béarnaise

This is a "close your eyes and you won't believe it doesn't have butter in it" substitute for the real thing. Great for entertaining those last minute guests who always seem to pop up when you least expect them. Goes well with beef or veal.

Simmer until thick.
Makes 1¼ cups.

*½ cup dry white wine*
*½ cup parsley sprigs*
*¼ cup white vinegar*
*1 small onion, quartered*
*2 large garlic cloves*
*1 tablespoon crushed, dried tarragon*
*¼ teaspoon crushed, dried chervil*
*⅛ teaspoon pepper*
*1 cup mayonnaise*
*Chopped parsley for garnish*

Blend all the ingredients, except for the mayonnaise, in a blender or food processor on high speed until smooth. Pour the mixture into a small saucepan and stir over medium heat until reduced to ⅓ cup. Strain and return the liquid to the saucepan. Add the mayonnaise, stirring constantly over medium heat until just warm. Serve garnished with chopped parsley. This recipe can be doubled or tripled. Can be made several hours in advance and reheated over a low flame while stirring.

## Mock Hollandaise

Fantastic over vegetables. Tastes as rich as if it had a pound of butter in it.

Simmer until thick.
Makes 1⅔ cups.

*1 cup mayonnaise*
*2 eggs*
*3 tablespoons lemon juice*
*½ teaspoon salt*
*½ teaspoon dry mustard*
*Paprika for garnish*

In a small saucepan, use a wire whisk to blend all the ingredients until smooth. Stir constantly over medium-low heat until thick (do not boil). Pour into a serving bowl or directly over vegetables, fish or poached eggs. Sprinkle with paprika. Serve immediately. Can be doubled or tripled. Can be made several hours in advance and reheated over a low flame while stirring.

TIP: Mayonnaise separates when it gets too cold. Keep it on the door of the refrigerator.

## Brown Gravy

It's brown, it's gravy, so have fun with it. I know gravy seems to be far more popular in the winter, but I make it in the middle of a heat wave just the same.

Makes 3–4 cups.

*¼ cup water*
*1 chopped onion*
*1 cup whole wheat flour*
*5½ cups water*
*½ cup soy sauce*

In a saucepan, combine the ¼ cup water and onion and heat, stirring occasionally, until the onion softens, about 5 minutes. Mix in the flour well and continue cooking another 3 minutes, stirring constantly. The flour and onions will clump together (this is okay). Add the remaining water and soy sauce and simmer another 5 minutes, stirring frequently. Remove the mixture from the heat.

Process the mixture in batches in a blender or food processor until the gravy is smooth. Place the gravy in a clean pot and simmer over medium heat, stirring frequently, until the gravy thickens, about 10–15 minutes. Season with fresh ground pepper to taste.

HINT: If the gravy fails to thicken to your satisfaction, you may want to add an extra thickener. Dissolve 2 tablespoons of cornstarch in ¼ cup cold water; gradually add to the gravy, stirring continuously until it is thick enough for serving.

## Enchilada Sauce

This is a very versatile sauce. Anything and everything Mexican goes with it.

Cook about 7 minutes.
Makes 4 cups.

*2 cups tomato sauce*
*3 cups water*
*¼ teaspoon garlic powder*
*½ teaspoon onion powder*
*3 tablespoons chili powder*
*4 tablespoons cornstarch*

In a large saucepan, combine all the ingredients and cook over medium heat, stirring constantly, until the mixture boils and thickens.

DAIRY AND MEAT OPTIONS: This is great over a bean- and cheese-filled burrito, or as a sauce over grilled chicken or fish.

## Champagne Cream Sauce

Makes a little more than 2 cups.

*6 egg yolks*
*1 cup sugar*
*1½ cups champagne, room temperature*

Combine the yolks and sugar over a double boiler. Cook over a low flame, whisking the mixture constantly for about 10 minutes, until the mixture begins to thicken. Before it turns to a thick custard, pour in the champagne all at once. As it foams up, whisk lightly and continue to stir as it thickens. Remove from the heat. Serve warm over chilled berries or over dessert pasta and top with additional berries.

OPTION: Substitute a sweet wine for the champagne.

## Orange Sauce

This versatile sauce can be used with both sweet and savory dishes. It is great over blintzes or soufflés.

Makes 1¼ cup.

*1 cup orange juice*
*½ cup sugar*
*1 tablespoon cornstarch*

Mix well all the ingredients in a saucepan. Heat over a medium flame, stirring constantly; let boil 1 minute, while continuing to stir. Remove from heat.

OPTIONS: If you add ¼ cup rice wine vinegar, you'll get a sweet and sour sauce, great for chicken or fish.

## Berry Berry Sauce

Delicious over fruit, ice creams, cake or anything else you can think of.

Makes 2 cups.

*2 cups strawberries*
*1 cup raspberries*
*1 cup blackberries*
*1 cup granulated sugar*
*2 teaspoons lemon juice*
*1 teaspoon grated lemon peel*

Place all the berries in a food processor. Process into a purée. Press the mixture through a fine sieve to remove seeds and place it into a saucepan. Add the sugar to the berries and mix well until the sugar is dissolved. Stir in the lemon juice and lemon peel. Bring the mixture to a boil, reduce the heat and simmer until the sauce yields 2 cups. Cool and serve.

TIP: This can be made several days in advance and stored in the refrigerator, or several weeks in advance and frozen. You can double or triple this recipe.

WARNING: This sauce will stain.

## Strawberry Coulis

When strawberries are in season, you can make a ton of this sauce and freeze it for when you crave berries in the middle of the winter.

Makes about 2 cups.

*2 cups strawberries*
*⅓ cup apple juice*
*3 tablespoons granulated sugar*

In a food processor, process the strawberries, apple juice and sugar. Pour the mixture into a saucepan and cook over low heat, simmering and stirring occasionally until the sauce is thick. Press the sauce through a sieve to remove seeds. Pour into a mixing bowl and cool.

## Apricot Raspberry Sauce

This is wonderful over that sponge cake that's gotten a little too hard, or as a topping for fresh fruit or sorbet.

Makes 2½–3 cups.

*8 peeled apricots*
*2 cups fresh or frozen raspberries*
*½ cup apple juice*
*2 tablespoons lemon juice*
*¼ cup granulated sugar*

Purée the apricots and raspberries in a food processor. Press the purée through a sieve (to remove seeds) and pour the liquid into a saucepan. Mix in well the remaining ingredients. Simmer, stirring occasionally and cook until the sauce thickens. Cool.

## Kiwi Mango Sauce

A good mango is worth its weight in gold. The combination of the mango and kiwi is an event not to be missed.

Makes 2½–3 cups.

*6 chopped kiwis*
*2 cups chopped mango*
*¼ cup granulated sugar*
*1½ tablespoons cornstarch*
*⅓ cup apple juice*

In a food processor, purée the kiwis with the mango. Press the fruit mixture through a sieve and pour into a small saucepan. Stir in the sugar. In a small bowl, mix the cornstarch with the apple juice and add it to the fruit mixture. Heat over a low flame, stirring occasionally. Cook until the sauce thickens. Cool.

## Salsa Vinaigrette

Let sit for at least 1 hour.
Makes ¾ cup.

*½ cup salsa*
*2 tablespoons vegetable oil*
*2 tablespoons fresh chopped parsley*

Place all the ingredients in a small jar with a lid. Shake well and then let sit before using. Great over salad greens, cooked cold potatoes, shredded cabbage or cold pasta.

## Guacamole Salad Dressing

Makes 2 cups.

*1 large avocado*
*1 tablespoon lemon juice*
*1 tablespoon very finely minced onion*
*⅛ tablespoon cayenne pepper*
*¼ teaspoon cumin*
*¼ cup mayonnaise (or more)*
*salt and pepper to taste*
*1 small tomato, seeded and chopped*

Peel avocado and mash in a glass bowl; immediately add lemon juice and mix well. Add onions and enough cayenne to make the taste sharp, but not hot. Add the cumin. Mix well. Add only enough mayonnaise to achieve the smoothness you prefer. Season with salt and pepper. Add the tomato. This recipe can be doubled.

## Honey Apricot Salad Dressing

This is great for Rosh Hashanah, when you just gotta have more honey.

Makes 2½ to 3 cups.

*¼ cup honey*
*11 oz. apricot nectar*
*2 teaspoons minced garlic*
*⅓ cup vegetable oil*
*½ cup raspberry vinegar (or red wine vinegar)*
*1½ teaspoons cornstarch*
*½ teaspoon ground ginger*
*¼ cup fresh basil*
*⅛ teaspoon salt*
*⅛ teaspoon black pepper*
*1 tablespoon sesame seeds*

Combine all ingredients, except the sesame seeds, in a medium saucepan and bring to a slow boil; simmer for 5 minutes. Cool; then add the sesame seeds and mix well. Refrigerate. Can be stored in the refrigerator for up to 10 days. This is great on fresh fruit or vegetable salads.

# Fruit Refreshers

Fruits, while intrinsically pareve and incredibly versatile, can also help you and your family stay healthy.

According to the USDA and just about every other health organization, everyone should consume at least 5 units of fruits and vegetables per day (and more if possible). Fruits are also a great source of vitamins and fiber. The only drawback to fruit is that sometimes the fruits aren't quite as ripe as you'd like them to be when you buy them. Try ripening your fruit in a closed paper bag for 2–3 days on the kitchen counter. Then you can enjoy the smell and anticipate the taste.

While there are many great fruit recipes, there isn't room in this chapter for all of them. The following recipes are the best of the best and are guaranteed to have everyone begging for seconds.

# Strawberries with Purée

A simple and easy dessert
that looks like a million bucks.
If fresh berries are available,
spoil yourself and buy as many
as you can. If you can't use them
right away, freeze them;
you can make jelly or jam with them
when you have the time.

Makes 4 servings.

*⅓ cup water*
*¼ cup sugar*
*1 cup blueberries*
*1 cup fresh or frozen raspberries*
*1 teaspoon lemon juice*
*2 cups strawberries*
*Non-dairy whipped topping for garnish*
*Mint sprigs for garnish*

In a small, heavy saucepan, bring the water and sugar to a boil, stirring until the sugar dissolves. Cool the syrup to room temperature, about 20 minutes. Meanwhile, purée the blueberries and raspberries in a blender or processor. Strain into a medium bowl, discarding the seeds. Stir in the syrup and lemon juice. Refrigerate until chilled.

Divide the strawberries among 4 dessert bowls and spoon ¼ cup of the purée on top of each portion. Garnish the berries with whipped topping and mint sprigs. In a separate dish, serve the remaining purée for additional topping.

NOTE: The purée can be prepared 2–3 days ahead of time.

# Pineapple Fruit Salad

This is like a trip to Hawaii
without having to pay the airfare.
It's got great eye-appeal and
is easy to make in large quantities.
So, if you have a Shabbos
where the entire family and
half the world is coming,
this is what you should be making.

Makes 8 servings.

*2 whole pineapples*
*2 coarsely chopped papayas*
*1½ cups seedless grapes*
*2 peeled and coarsely chopped apples*
*½ cup pecan halves*
*2 sliced bananas*
*½ cup lime juice*
*Salad greens for garnish*
*2 quartered limes for garnish*

Cut the pineapple lengthwise into quarters; cut away and discard the core. Remove the fruit by carefully cutting between it and the outer skin. Cut the pineapple into chunks and combine with the other fruit and lime juice in a bowl. Gently toss and chill. Make individual servings by arranging the fruit salad on the salad greens and topping with a lime garnish.

## Spiced Peaches

Perfect as a quickie side dish.
It lasts for weeks in the refrigerator,
so you may want to plan ahead
and make several batches.

Simmer for 10 minutes.
Makes 4 servings.

*4 cups canned cling peaches with juice*
*1⅓ cups sugar*
*1 cup cider vinegar*
*4 sticks cinnamon*
*2 teaspoons whole cloves*

Drain peaches, reserving their syrup and put the peaches in a large bowl. In a large saucepan, combine the peach syrup, sugar, vinegar, cinnamon and cloves; bring to a boil, lower heat and simmer. Pour the hot syrup over the peach halves and let them cool. Chill thoroughly before serving. This recipe can be doubled or tripled.

## Watermelon Fantasy

Nothing beats watermelon on
a hot, summer day!
In the part of Indiana where I live,
fresh-picked watermelon is available
from local farms and we go through
at least two a week!

Makes 6–8 servings.

*1 small watermelon*
*1 cantaloupe*
*2 bananas*
*1½ cups pineapple chunks*
*1½ cups lemon-lime carbonated drink*

Cut the watermelon lengthwise in half; scoop balls from its center with a melon scoop. Halve the cantaloupe and remove its seeds. Then scoop balls from the cantaloupe. Cut the bananas into bite-size pieces and drain the pineapple chunks. Combine the fruit in a scraped half-watermelon shell; toss lightly. Cover and chill until ready to serve. Pour the chilled lemon-lime drink over the fruit and serve immediately.

## Fruit Salad

This is a wonderful salad in the winter, when the really good "fresh" fruits are either too expensive or not available.

### Makes 4 servings.

¾ cup pineapple chunks, drained
¼ cup pitted dates
1¼ medium carrots, thinly sliced
¾ sliced orange
¾ sliced banana
1 tablespoon plus 2 teaspoons honey
2½ teaspoons white wine vinegar
2½ teaspoons lime juice
1½ tablespoons vegetable oil
¾ teaspoon grated lime zest

Combine the pineapple, dates, carrots, orange and banana in a large bowl. Combine the remaining ingredients in a jar with a tight-fitting lid. Shake the jar vigorously and pour the dressing over the fruit. Add the bananas last, as they brown quickly without the dressing. Chill until ready to serve. You can double or triple this recipe.

OPTION: Add chopped figs, sliced almonds and/or mangos.

## Citrus Salad

### Makes 6 servings.

4 lemons
4 limes
4 oranges
1⅓ cups sugar
⅔ cup water
2 cups grapefruit segments
1 cup pineapple chunks
1 cup mango chunks

Remove the rind from the lemons, limes and oranges using a vegetable peeler; then cut the rind into thin julienne strips. Juice the lemons, limes and oranges and strain the juice to remove the seeds. Pour the juice into a non-reactive saucepan, add the fruit rind, sugar and water and bring to a boil over medium-high heat. Reduce the heat to medium-low and simmer about 10 minutes or until the mixture becomes syrupy. Mix together the grapefruit, pineapple and mango and spoon into 6 dessert bowls. Pour the syrup over the fruit and chill before serving.

# Melon Balls 'n Rum

More fun with fruit
for the over-21 crowd.

Makes 8–10 servings.

*⅓ cup water*
*⅓ cup sugar*
*½ cup light rum*
*⅓ cup fresh-squeezed lime juice*
*1 teaspoon grated lime peel*
*¼ small watermelon*
*1 cantaloupe*
*1 honeydew melon*
*1 cup fresh blueberries*

In a small saucepan, bring the water to a boil. Stir in the sugar and simmer for 3 minutes. Add the rum and simmer for another 2 minutes. Remove from the the heat, allow to cool 10–15 minutes and stir in the lime juice and the grated lime peel. Cut the melons into balls with a melon scoop and combine them with the blueberries in a serving bowl. Pour the syrup over the fruit and mix gently. Cover and chill for several hours before serving.

# Peach Cranberry Crumble

Different and easy.
A great dessert in the winter.

Bake at 350° for 1 hour.
Makes 6–8 servings.

*2 cups uncooked oatmeal*
*¾ cup all-purpose flour*
*¼ cup ground pecans*
*¾ cup brown sugar*
*1 teaspoon cinnamon*
*½ teaspoon salt*
*½ cup oil*
*1½ cups whole cranberry sauce*
*2 cups canned sliced peaches, drained*

Preheat oven. In a large bowl, combine the oatmeal, flour, ground pecans, sugar, cinnamon and salt. Add the oil and mix well until crumbly. Grease an 8-inch square pan. Spread half of the crumb mixture in the pan. In a separate bowl, combine the peaches and cranberry sauce. Pour the fruit mixture into the pan over the crumb mixture. Spread the remaining crumb mixture over the top of the fruit. Bake uncovered. Serve hot.

111

## Mixed-Up Fruit Salad

The options are endless!

Refrigerate several hours.
Makes 6–8 servings.

*2 seedless oranges or grapefruits*
*2 peeled apples or pears*
*2 sliced bananas*
*2 cups chopped pitted dates*
*1 cup chopped dried figs or apricots*
*1 cup chopped almonds or pecans*
*1 cup orange juice*
*Crushed almonds or grated coconut for garnish*

Place all the fruit you choose in a serving bowl. Pour the orange juice over the fruit and mix gently. Cover and chill before serving. Garnish with almonds or coconut.

TIP: For an easy-to-make fruit salad dressing, mix together 1 teaspoon grated orange rind, ⅓ cup orange juice and 1 cup pareve sour cream.

## Raspberry Cream Fruit Salad

So much better than
plain tossed salad!

Makes about 1½ cups dressing.

*⅔ cup pareve cream cheese*
*1 tablespoon brown sugar*
*½ teaspoon ginger*
*1 tablespoon red wine vinegar*
*1 cup crushed raspberries*
*Chopped fresh peaches, nectarines and pears*
*Salad greens for garnish*

In a small bowl, combine the pareve cream cheese, brown sugar, ginger and vinegar. Blend until smooth. Stir in the crushed raspberries and mix well. Chill. Place the salad greens on individual salad plates and arrange the fresh fruit on top. Drizzle 1–2 tablespoons dressing on top of each portion and serve.

TIP: To make lettuce or salad greens crisp, add 1 tablespoon of vinegar to a pan of water and let them soak for 15 minutes.

# Apricot Nut Spread

Better than butter.

Makes 3–4 cups.

*2½ cups fresh, ripe apricots*
*2 cups sugar*
*¼ cup orange juice or orange flavored*
*liqueur*
*¾ cup diced dried apricots*
*1 cup chopped walnuts*

In a large, heavy saucepan, combine the pitted fresh apricots with sugar and orange juice. Cook over low heat, stirring occasionally, until the apricots soften and lose their shape. Purée the mixture in a food processor. Transfer the purée to a saucepan and continue to cook on low heat, stirring often, for 6–8 minutes, or until it looks like spaghetti sauce; this mixture darkens as it reduces. Add the dried apricots and nuts and simmer slowly for an additional ½ hour. Cool and cover. Store in the refrigerator.

NOTE: This spread will keep for several weeks.

# Cranberry Sauce with Amaretto

Something special you can do with cranberries.
Serve over baked apples.

Makes about 4 cups.

*2 cups sugar*
*1 cup water*
*4 cups raw cranberries*
*⅓ cup orange marmalade*
*Juice of 2 lemons*
*½ cup blanched whole almonds*
*⅓ cup amaretto (almond liqueur)*

Bring the sugar and water to a boil. Turn down heat and simmer for 15 minutes. Add the cranberries to the syrup and simmer for another 5 minutes, or until the skins burst. Remove from the heat. Mix in the marmalade and lemon juice. Allow to cool. Stir in the almonds and amaretto. Chill before serving.

MEAT OPTION: Serve with roasted chicken or turkey.

# *Desserts & Frostings*

Welcome to Dessert Central. Please make sure that you check your calorie-counter at the door. Be sure to come with your belt buckle loosened and your tastebuds ready.

A good dessert is a thing of beauty. And beauty, as we all know, is truly in the eyes of the beholder. A dessert can be chocolate or not, plain or frosted, with nuts or without. However, whichever type of dessert you choose, you can be guaranteed that within 15 minutes of taking your treat out of the oven, everyone will find an excuse to wander into the kitchen for a look or taste.

So in honor of those of us who would like to eat dessert first, I offer the following recipes. They are all outstanding examples of what you can create when your tastebuds go into overdrive and your imagination is limitless.

# Brown Sugar Pear Tart

The pecan crust from this tart is so good, you'll start using it for other desserts.

Bake at 375° for 15–20 minutes.
Makes 6–8 Servings.

### Crust:
1⅓ cups all-purpose flour
⅓ cup packed brown sugar
⅓ cup finely chopped pecans
½ teaspoon ground nutmeg
½ teaspoon grated lemon peel
⅔ cup firm margarine

### Filling:
3–5 medium pears (2 pounds), peeled
½ cup packed brown sugar
2 tablespoons all-purpose flour
½ teaspoon ground cinnamon

### Garnish:
Chopped pears (optional)
Red seedless grapes (optional)
Pecan halves (optional)
Lemon zest (optional)

### To prepare crust:

Preheat oven. In a large bowl, mix all ingredients EXCEPT the margarine. Cut in the margarine until mixture is crumbly. Press the dough firmly and evenly against the bottom of an ungreased 11-inch tart pan. Bake 8 minutes and then remove from oven and cool.

### To prepare filling:

Cut each pear in half lengthwise and remove the core. Place each pear (cut side down) on a cutting surface. Cut the pear halves crosswise into thin slices. Lift each pear half with a spatula and arrange on cooled crust, separating and overlapping the slices (retain the pear shape) to cover the surface of the crust, leaving an open area in the center.

In a medium-size bowl, combine the brown sugar, flour and cinnamon; sprinkle the mixture over the pears. Bake until the crust is golden brown and the pears are tender.

Garnish by placing chopped pears, grapes, pecan halves and lemon zest in the center of the tart.

# 'Lotta Lime Pie

Sort of like a Key Lime Pie,
except that you can use any kind of
lime that you like.

Bake crust at 375° for 8 minutes.
Refrigerate pie overnight.
Makes 6–8 servings.

### Crust:
*1¼ cups graham cracker crumbs*
*5 tablespoons melted margarine, cooled*
*¼ cup brown sugar*
*1 tablespoon grated lime zest*
*Pinch of salt*

### Filling:
*4 egg yolks, lightly beaten*
*½ cup plus 2 tablespoons sugar*
*⅓ cup fresh lime juice*
*2 teaspoons grated lime zest*
*2¼ cups non-dairy whipping cream*
*1 teaspoon vanilla extract*

Preheat oven. Butter a 9-inch pie plate. In a large bowl, combine the crust ingredients and stir until the mixture lumps together. Using a fork, press the mixture into the bottom and sides of the pie plate. Bake; set aside on a wire rack until completely cool.

Combine the egg yolks, ½ cup sugar and lime juice in the top of a double boiler. Cook over low heat, stirring occasionally with a wooden spoon until the mixture coats the back of the spoon (about 15 minutes); stir in the lime zest. Remove from the heat and chill until the filling thickens to the consistency of a partially set custard.

Whip 1½ cups of non-dairy creamer so that it forms peaks. Fold the chilled filling into the non-dairy creamer.

Spoon the mixture into the crust and smooth. Cover with plastic wrap and chill.

Just before serving, whip the remaining non-dairy creamer with the vanilla and 2 tablespoons sugar until the cream forms stiff peaks. Spread the topping over the pie filling.

DAIRY OPTION: Substitute butter for the margarine and whipped cream for the non-dairy creamer.

## No-Egg Chocolate Mousse Pie

For those who have to limit eggs.

Freeze for at least 2–3 hours.
Makes 6–8 servings.

*1 cup marshmallow cream*
*2 squares bittersweet chocolate*
*¼ cup non-dairy creamer*
*Dash of salt*
*1 teaspoon vanilla extract*
*1½ cups whipped non-dairy topping*
*9-inch graham cracker pie crust*
*Chocolate chips or shavings for garnish*

In a saucepan, mix the marshmallow cream, chocolate and non-dairy creamer and cook over a very low flame until melted and thick (or melt in a microwave for 2 minutes, stirring after 1 minute). Add the salt and vanilla, mix well and let cool in the refrigerator 30 minutes. Fold in the whipped topping and then pour it into the pre-made pie shell. (You can use a regular pie shell that's already cooked.) Put the pie in the freezer in the pie shell and freeze. Garnish with chocolate chips, chocolate shavings, or extra whipped topping.

### Graham Cracker Pie Crust:
*8 parve graham crackers*
*¼ cup sugar*
*2 tablespoons margarine*

Process graham crackers in food processor until they are fine. Add the sugar and margarine and blend until smooth. Spread the crumb mixture into a pie pan and bake for 10 minutes at 350°. Remove from heat and cool. Makes 1 pie shell.

## Apricot Pie

This is a cross between a cake and a pie and is guaranteed to go with everything.

Bake at 350° for 30 minutes.
Makes 8 servings.

*2 cups canned apricot halves*
*2 eggs*
*¾ cup sugar*
*4 ounces melted margarine, cooled*
*1 teaspoon vanilla*
*1 cup all-purpose flour, sifted*
*1 teaspoon baking powder*
*¼ cup cinnamon and sugar (see Note, p. 27,*
*Morning Glory Muffins)*

Preheat oven. Grease a 10-inch-round pie plate and set it aside. Drain the apricots and lay them on paper towels. In a mixing bowl, combine the eggs and sugar; beat till light and creamy and pale lemon-colored, about 8–10 minutes. Fold in the margarine and vanilla, then fold in the sifted flour and baking powder. Pour the batter into the pie plate and arrange the apricot halves on top of the batter, rounded side up. While still warm, sprinkle with the cinnamon/sugar mixture. Serve warm. Do not double this recipe.

# Basic Pie Crust Dough

Makes one pie crust with a little extra for decoration.

*1 cup all-purpose flour*
*½ teaspoon salt*
*⅓ cup shortening*
*2–3 tablespoons ice water or orange juice*

In a large bowl, combine the flour and salt. Cut in the shortening until the mixture resembles small, crumbly pebbles. Sprinkle the water or juice over the top and work it into the crumbly mixture until a smooth dough begins to form. Shape the dough into a ball and then roll it out with a rolling pin into a circle ⅛-inch thick and 13 inches in diameter. Fit the dough into the pie pan and then trim the edges to fit. Then, shape and build up the edges by folding under the extra dough and pinching together. Fill and bake according to individual pie recipe.

TIP: Pastry will come out flakier if a few drops of vinegar are added to the cold water.

# Another Pie Crust Dough

Makes 2 9-inch pie crusts plus extra for decoration.

*5 cups all-purpose flour*
*½ teaspoon salt*
*1 pound shortening*
*1¼–1½ cups cold 7-Up soda (or ginger ale)*

In a bowl, combine the flour and salt. Cut in the shortening until the mixture resembles small, crumbly pebbles. Pour in 1¼ cups soda (more, if needed) and work it into the crumbly mixture until a smooth dough begins to form. Do not over-mix. Divide the dough in half, forming 2 balls. Roll out with a rolling pin on a floured cutting board. Proceed as instructed for Basic Pie Crust Dough in the previous recipe.

# Other Kinds of Crusts

Bake at 375° for 7–8 minutes.
Makes 1 pie shell.

### Graham Cracker:
1⅓ cups graham cracker crumbs
¼ cup sugar
¼ cup melted margarine

### Chocolate Cookie:
1⅓ cups chocolate cookie crumbs
3 tablespoons melted margarine

### Vanilla Cookie:
1⅓ cups vanilla cookie crumbs
¼ cup melted margarine

### Corn Flakes:
1⅓ cups crushed corn flakes
2 tablespoons sugar
¼ cup melted margarine

### Nutty Crust:
1⅓ cups ground nuts (walnuts, pecans,
almonds, etc.)
¼ cup sugar
¼ cup melted margarine

Preheat oven. In a bowl, combine your favorite cookies, nuts or flakes with the sugar and margarine required. Set aside 3–4 tablespoons for topping. Press the remaining crumb-sugar-margarine mixture into the bottom and sides of a 9-inch pie pan. Bake. Cool, fill and top with the remaining crumbs. These recipes can be doubled or tripled.

NOTE: You can add cinnamon or ground nuts to any of the crusts. Simply add a little more margarine to compensate.

# Gingerbread Crust

Bake at 375° for 25 minutes.
Makes 1 crust.

1½ cups all-purpose flour
3 tablespoons firmly packed brown sugar
2 teaspoons ground ginger
2½ teaspoons ground cinnamon
¾ teaspoon ground allspice
½ teaspoon salt
½ cup cold margarine, cut into pieces
1 large egg yolk
2 tablespoons dark molasses
raw rice for weighting the crust

Preheat oven. In a food processor, process together the flour, brown sugar, ginger, cinnamon, allspice and salt. Add the margarine and blend until it resembles coarse meal. In a small bowl, stir together the egg yolk and the molasses. Then add the egg mixture to the flour mixture and blend until it is combined well, but still crumbly. Turn the mixture out into a 10-inch tart pan with a fluted removable rim, and press it onto the bottom and up the side of the pan. Chill the crust for 30 minutes. Poke it with a fork 3 or 4 times and line the inside of the crust with foil. Fill the foil with the rice. Bake the crust in the lower half of the oven for 15 minutes. Remove the foil and rice carefully and bake the crust for another 10 minutes. Let the crust cool in the pan on a rack. Fill with a precooked filling.

## Puff Pastry

Yes, great stuff is available in the freezer section of your local grocery, but yours will taste better.
This dough is perfect for wrapping beef and chicken (Wellington), fruit (strudels) or vegetables (knishes); or bake separately and use for making Napoleons.

Bake at 350° for 12–15 minutes.
Makes 2 pounds.

*4½ cups all-purpose flour*
*2 teaspoons salt*
*1 tablespoon margarine or shortening*
*1½ cups ice water*
*2 tablespoons white vinegar*
*1 pound margarine or shortening*
*2 tablespoons all-purpose flour*

Mix the 4½ cups flour and salt in a bowl. Cut 1 tablespoon of margarine into the flour. Make a well (hole) in the center of the mixture and add the water and vinegar. Mix and then turn the dough onto a working surface (wood is nice but marble is better). Knead for about 10 minutes, adding very little flour (only if needed). Chill 30 minutes.

Meanwhile, blend 1 pound margarine and 2 tablespoons flour and shape into a 4-inch square. Chill 20 minutes.

Roll out the dough into a ½-inch thick square. Center the margarine plaque on top of the dough and fold the sides of the dough over the margarine, covering it and overlapping the dough edges a little. Press the edges together with a rolling pin. Roll out the dough to 1-inch thick. Fold in thirds like a letter. Roll out and fold again. Wrap in plastic wrap, cover with a damp cloth and chill 30 minutes. Repeat the rolling and folding, as before, 2 more times. You will have rolled and folded 6 times altogether. To bake: Roll out, cut to desired shape and fill.

NOTE: Sprinkle flour on the working surface and rolling pin every time you roll out the dough. If the dough tears a little while rolling out, you can patch it with a little dough. If the holes are small just leave as is. Try to work with this dough in a cold environment. You may freeze it up to 6 months or keep it in the refrigerator for up to 3 days.

## Basic Custard

A classic that always comes out perfectly. Great for filling fruit tarts and all kinds of cakes.

Makes about 1½ cups.

*½ cup sugar*
*4 egg yolks*
*1 cup non-dairy creamer*
*1 teaspoon vanilla*

In a large saucepan, whisk the sugar and yolks together over a low flame. Gradually whisk in the non-dairy creamer and vanilla. Increase to a medium heat, stirring constantly, until the mixture is smooth and thick.

OPTION: Substitute almond or rum for the vanilla.

# Vanilla Cream Filling

A never-fail show stopper
that can be used to fill tarts, pies
or cakes. Check out the different
variations that can jazz up
even the most boring desserts.

Makes about 1 cup.

*⅓ cup sugar*
*2 tablespoons cornstarch*
*¼ teaspoon salt*
*1 cup non-dairy creamer*
*1 egg*
*1 teaspoon vanilla*

In a saucepan, whisk together the sugar, cornstarch and salt. Gradually whisk in the non-dairy creamer, egg and vanilla. Cook the mixture over medium heat, whisking constantly until the mixture is smooth and thick, about 4–5 minutes. Remove the mixture from the heat and cover with wax paper (or plastic wrap) so that it touches the top of the mixture. Let cool and then refrigerate. This recipe can be doubled.

NOTE: Keeps in the refrigerator for 2 days or in the freezer for up to 3 weeks.

### Coffee Cream Filling:

Substitute the non-dairy creamer with 2 teaspoons instant coffee mixed with 1 cup of hot water.

### Chocolate Cream Filling:

Add 3 tablespoons unsweetened cocoa to the dry ingredients.

# Lemon Custard

This is one of those recipes
that everyone begs for.
This custard can be used as a tart
or jelly roll filling,
or served in small dessert bowls.

Makes 1 cup.

*1 cup sugar*
*½ cup fresh lemon juice*
*1 tablespoon lemon zest*
*2 eggs*

In a mixing bowl, combine all the ingredients. Beat with a mixer at high speed until smooth. Pour the mixture into a saucepan and cook, stirring constantly with a whisk, over medium heat until just bubbling. The mixture should be thick and smooth. Remove from the heat to cool and thicken. Pour into a storage container, cover and refrigerate. This recipe can be doubled.

NOTE: This will keep up to a week in the refrigerator or 2 months in the freezer.

# Coconut Custard Cream

This is an eye-popping substitute for a classic custard filling and so rich it carries its own gold card. Wonderful over fruit, especially pineapple and mangos. Not recommended for cholesterol watchers.

Makes 4 servings.

*1 cup sugar*
*¼ cup water*
*6 egg yolks*
*1 cup coconut cream or coconut milk*
*A few drops vanilla*

In a saucepan, mix together the sugar and water and cook over medium heat until you get a thick syrup. Set aside and let cool. In a bowl, blend together the yolks, coconut cream and vanilla. Stir in the cooled syrup and mix well. Pour the mixture into a double boiler and simmer, stirring well, until the mixture coats the spoon. Let cool and then chill.

TIP: To cool a hot dish in a hurry, place it in a pan of cool salted water.

# Orange Custard

So simple that you'll wish you'd tried it sooner. So good that you'll want it every day. Great for filling fruit tarts and all kinds of cakes.

Makes about 1½ cups.

*½ cup sugar*
*4 egg yolks*
*1 cup orange juice*

In a large saucepan, whisk together the sugar and the yolks. Gradually whisk in the orange juice and simmer over medium heat, stirring constantly, until the mixture is smooth and thick.

NOTE: Use sparingly; this is a very sweet filling.

# Almond Fruit Torte

Easy, elegant and beautiful.

Bake at 375° for 20–25 minutes.
Makes 8 servings.

¼ cup plus 3 tablespoons softened
margarine
½ cup sugar
2 eggs
1 cup ground blanched or toasted* almonds
⅛ teaspoon salt
¼ cup melted red raspberry preserves,
strained
2 cups strawberries, halved lenghtwise
2 pears, halved lengthwise and cut into
thin slices
1 kiwi, cut crosswise into thin slices
¼ cup melted apricot preserves, strained

Preheat oven. Combine the margarine and sugar in a mixing bowl. Beat with a mixer until light and fluffy. Add eggs, one at a time, mixing thoroughly after each addition. Add almonds and salt and again mix thoroughly. Line a 9-inch round cake pan with wax paper and grease with margarine. Spread the batter in the pan. Bake until golden brown. Place the torte on a rack to cool.

When cool, invert the torte onto a serving platter. Carefully pull off the waxed paper. Brush the torte with the raspberry preserves. Arrange the strawberries, pears and kiwi in a circular pattern (any way you like) on top. Brush with the apricot preserves and chill. Do not double this recipe.

DAIRY OPTION: Spread a thin layer of vanilla pudding or custard on top of the torte after the raspberry jam layer and then lay the fruit on top of the pudding.

*To toast almonds, spread in an ungreased baking pan. Place in a 350° oven and bake 5–10 minutes or until lightly brown; stir once or twice. Almonds will brown slightly more once removed from the oven.

# Chocolate Almond Torte with Strawberry Sauce

Bake at 300° for about 1½ hours.
Makes 16 servings.

1¼ cups sugar
1 cup softened margarine
4 eggs, separated
2¼ cups sliced almonds
¾ cup plus 1 tablespoon unsweetened chocolate

**Sauce:**
2 cups frozen, unsweetened strawberries
1 cup sugar

Fresh strawberries for garnish

Preheat oven. Line the bottom of a 9-inch springform pan with wax paper; grease the paper and set aside. In a mixing bowl, cream together the sugar and margarine until fluffy. Mix in the egg yolks. In a food processor, finely grind the almonds and chocolate. Stir the chocolate and almonds into the sugar mixture. In a separate bowl, beat the egg whites to stiff peaks; mix ⅓ whites into the batter and gently fold in the remaining whites. Spread the batter into the pan, smoothing the top. Bake until the top springs back. Cool for 10 minutes before releasing from the pan.

### To prepare sauce:

Thaw the strawberries and purée in a blender. Transfer the strawberries to a small saucepan, stir in the sugar and heat. Simmer 3 minutes. Cover and cool.

### To serve:

Pour sauce on the serving plate. Place the torte on top. Garnish the top of the torte with fresh strawberries.

# Cherry Walnut Bars

Bake at 350° for 20 minutes.
Makes 2½ dozen.

2¼ cups all-purpose flour
½ cup granulated sugar
1 cup softened margarine
2 eggs
1 cup firmly packed brown sugar
½ teaspoon salt
½ teaspoon baking powder
1 teaspoon vanilla extract
1 4-ounce jar maraschino cherries
½ cup chopped walnuts
½ cup flaked coconut
1 teaspoon margarine
1 cup confectioners' sugar

Preheat oven. In a bowl, mix flour, sugar and margarine until crumbly. Press the mixture into a 9x13-inch baking pan. Bake for 20 minutes or until light brown. Beat together the eggs, brown sugar, salt, baking powder and vanilla. Drain and chop the cherries, saving the liquid. Add the cherries, nuts and coconut to the egg mixture. Mix well, pour over crust and bake.

Combine 1 teaspoon of margarine and the confectioners' sugar with enough liquid from the cherries to make the mixture spreadable, but not too thin. Spread the frosting over the bars after they have cooled. Sprinkle coconut on top when icing is set. Cut into pieces.

# Oatmeal Date Bars

Fiber-filled and taste great!

Bake at 325° for about 30–35 minutes.
Makes 32 squares.

### Filling:

*2 cups chopped dates*
*Grated rind of ½ orange*
*⅓ cup cold water*
*2 tablespoons orange juice*
*2 tablespoons brown sugar*
*1 teaspoon lemon juice*

### Crust:

*1½ cups all-purpose flour*
*1 teaspoon baking powder*
*½ teaspoon baking soda*
*¼ teaspoon salt*
*1 cup soft margarine*
*1 cup firmly packed brown sugar*
*1½ cups oats*

You need to make the filling first. In a medium saucepan, combine the dates, water, orange rind and brown sugar. Cook over medium heat until thick and smooth, stirring constantly. Remove from the heat and add fruit juices. Mix well and set aside to let cool. It must be cool before you spread it.

Preheat oven. In a bowl, combine the flour, baking powder, baking soda and salt. Add the margarine and mix it in with a fork (you can do this in a food processor, too). Add the brown sugar and oats. Mix well (again with a fork or food processor). Spread half the crumbs in a greased shallow 9x13-inch pan and pat to smooth. Cover with cooled filling, spreading

evenly and then layer the remaining crumbs on top. Pat smooth. Bake. Increase heat to 350° for an additional 5 minutes, to lightly brown the top. Cut in squares while hot and allow the bars to cool in the pan.

# Peanut Butter Cup Bars

These are even better than the candy bar.

Refrigerate for 2 hours.
Makes 8–10 servings.

*1 cup graham cracker crumbs*
*½ cup melted margarine*
*2 cups powdered sugar*
*⅔ cup peanut butter*
*1 teaspoon vanilla*

### Topping:

*1 cup chocolate chips, melted*
*1 tablespoon margarine*

In a bowl, combine the cookie ingredients and press the mixture into a greased 8x8-inch pan. Place the topping ingredients in a microwave-safe bowl and carefully microwave on high to melt or melt in a double boiler for 3–4 minutes. Using a spatula, spread the chocolate mixture over the top of the cookie, covering the entire surface. Refrigerate and then cut into squares.

## Sour Cherry Bars

Pucker up for this tangy
and sweet bar cookie.
Fresh cherries give it a subtler taste.

Bake at 350° for 45 minutes.
Makes 16 bar cookies.

### Crust:

*1½ cups all-purpose flour*
*½ cup cold margarine*
*5 tablespoons powdered sugar*

### Filling:

*3 eggs*
*1 cup sugar*
*1 cup brown sugar*
*1 teaspoon baking powder*
*½ cup all-purpose flour*
*3 cups pitted sour cherries, drained or fresh*

Preheat oven. In a bowl, mix together well the flour, margarine and powdered sugar (you can alternatively use a food processor). Don't let the crust mixture become too warm, or it will become sticky and hard to handle. Pat the dough into a 9x13-inch pan. Bake for 15 minutes and then set aside.

If you are using a food processor to make the filling, pour all the filling ingredients except the cherries into the work bowl of the processor and process until well-mixed. Add the sour cherries and chop up by bursts of the on/off switch. Don't chop too fine or the fruit will become too mushy. If using an electric mixer or mixing by hand, first mix together all the filling ingredients, except for the fruit. Then chop the cherries into small pieces and stir into the mixture. Pour the filling into the partially baked crust and bake.

NOTE: You can use rhubarb, apricots, peaches or plums instead of the cherries. If, however, you decide to use berries, leave the fruit whole, as the juice adds too much liquid to the batter.

## Coffee Brownies

If I could have a cup
of these brownies every morning...

Bake at 325° for 30–35 minutes.
Makes 8 servings.

*¾ cup margarine*
*3 squares unsweetened chocolate*
*1½ cups sugar*
*1 tablespoon instant coffee*
*1 teaspoon vanilla*
*3 eggs*
*¾ cup all-purpose flour*
*½ teaspoon salt*

Over a low flame, in a double boiler or in the microwave, melt the margarine and chocolate together. When it's smooth add the sugar, coffee and vanilla. Mix well. When the mixture is cool (I know it's hard to wait) add the eggs, flour and salt. Fold in gently and pour into a 9x9-inch pan. Bake. You can bake it a little longer if you don't particularly like a gooey brownie.

# Rice Pudding

This may be the ultimate
in comfort foods.

Bake at 350° for 35–40 minutes.
Makes 4 servings.

*1 cup cooked rice*
*2 cups non-dairy creamer or rice milk*
*1 tablespoon cashew butter or other nut*
*butter (optional)\**
*2 eggs*
*½ cup sugar*
*½ teaspoon vanilla*
*¼ cup raisins, plumped in a little water*
*Dash cinnamon*

Preheat oven. In a saucepan, simmer the rice and non-dairy creamer together for 5–10 minutes. Add the nut butter and mix well. Remove from the heat. In a separate bowl, beat the eggs; add the sugar, vanilla, raisins and cinnamon, mixing well. Mix the egg mixture into the rice mixture and pour into a greased glass baking dish. Sprinkle a little more cinnamon on the top. Bake uncovered. This recipe can be doubled.

\* Peanut butter is too strong a taste to use unless you really love it.

# Banana Pasta

Another great dessert pasta!

Cook in boiling water for 3 minutes.
Makes 4–6 servings.

*1 cup (about 2) mashed bananas*
*⅓ cup granulated sugar*
*1 teaspoon vanilla extract*
*1 egg*
*2 cups all-purpose flour*
*Ice water, as needed*

In a bowl, mix together the banana, sugar, vanilla and egg. Blend in the flour. Knead the dough into a smooth ball (add small amounts of ice water, if required). Knead another 2–3 minutes, then allow the dough to rest for 15 minutes. Roll out the dough. Lightly dust with flour, fold in thirds and roll out again. Repeat 5 or 6 times. Pass through a pasta machine or cut by hand into thin strips. Cook the pasta in unsalted, boiling water. Drain and apportion into warmed plates. Serves 4–6. Serve with a fruit sauce or sweet wine sauce (see pp. 103–105 for example).

## Cocoa Pasta with Honey and Pistachios

Pasta for dessert may sound weird, but this is really a great dessert! Try any kind of sauce you like (except maybe tomato).

Cook in boiling water for 3 minutes. Makes 4 servings.

**Pasta:**

*3 cups all-purpose flour*
*½ cup cocoa*
*2 tablespoons granulated sugar*
*Pinch cinnamon*
*4 eggs*
*½ teaspoon vanilla extract*

**Sauce:**

*½ cup good quality, clear honey*
*½ cup chopped pistachio nuts*

In a large bowl, sift the flour with the cocoa. Stir in the sugar and cinnamon. Add the eggs and vanilla extract; mix together until you have a smooth dough. Roll out the dough on a floured surface until ⅛ inch thick. With a pastry wheel, cut the dough into strips ¾ inch wide and about 7 inches long. You can alternatively use a pasta machine to roll the dough out into the ribbons.

Cook the pasta in unsalted, boiling water. Drain and apportion into 4 warmed plates. Drizzle generous amounts of honey over the pasta and sprinkle pistachio nuts over each serving.

## Cocoa Pasta 2

Cook in boiling water for 3 minutes. Makes 4–6 servings.

*2 cups semolina flour*
*2 tablespoons cocoa*
*¼ cup granulated sugar*
*1 teaspoon vanilla sugar*
*3 beaten eggs*
*Ice water, if needed*

Sift together the flour, cocoa and sugar. In a medium bowl, mix the vanilla sugar with the eggs; stir in the flour mixture slowly to the eggs and knead it into a smooth ball (add small amounts of ice water, if required) Knead the dough for another 2–3 minutes, then allow the dough to rest for 15 minutes. Roll out the dough, lightly dust with flour, fold in thirds and roll out again. Repeat 5 or 6 times. Pass through a pasta machine or cut by hand to the desired size. If processed by hand, simply roll the dough and cut into thin strips for noodles. Cook the pasta in unsalted, boiling water. Drain; apportion into warmed serving plates. Serve with a fruit sauce or sweet wine sauce (see pp. 103–105 for example).

TIP: To make vanilla sugar, bury a length of vanilla bean in 4–5 cups sugar within an airtight jar and let sit for 3–5 days. Remove the bean and keep sealed until needed for baking. Keeps for several weeks.

# Strawberry Mousse

This is an outstanding dessert that takes only about a ½ hour to prepare.

Makes 6–8 servings.

*¼ cup fresh orange juice*
*2½ teaspoons unflavored kosher gelatin*
*1 egg*
*1 egg yolk*
*3 tablespoons sugar*
*1 cup hulled fresh strawberries*
*1 tablespoon framboise, creme de cassis or dark rum*
*⅓ cup non-dairy whipped topping, whipped to soft peaks*
*Sliced strawberries for garnish*
*Minced unsalted pistachios and/or fresh mint leaves for garnish*

Lightly oil one 3-cup mold (or two 1-cup soufflé dishes fitted with foil collars). Pour the orange juice into a cup; sprinkle with gelatin and let stand until the liquid is absorbed, about 5 minutes. Meanwhile, combine the whole egg, egg yolk and sugar in a medium-size bowl. Using an electric mixer, beat at high speed until the mixture becomes thick and forms slowly dissolving ribbons when the beaters are lifted, about 5–7 minutes. Set the mixture aside.

Combine the strawberries and framboise in a food processor or blender and purée until smooth. Set the cup with the gelatin mixture in a small pan of hot water and place over low heat until the gelatin is completely dissolved and clear. Stir the gelatin mixture into the egg mixture. Fold in the puréed strawberries. Set the bowl in a larger bowl of ice water and stir gently with a rubber spatula until the mixture is almost set, about 10 minutes. Fold in the whipped topping. Pour into the prepared dish and refrigerate until set. If using a mold, invert the mousse onto a platter before serving. Garnish the top with strawberries, pistachios and mint.

# Chocolate Ice Cream

Close your eyes when you're eating this and you'll think it's the real thing.

Makes 6 servings.

*3 eggs, separated*
*⅓ cup sugar*
*4 cups non-dairy whipped cream*
*3 tablespoons cocoa*
*1 tablespoon vanilla*

Using a mixer on high speed, beat the egg whites until foamy and almost double in volume. Slowly beat in the sugar until the whites form soft peaks. Set aside. In a separate bowl, beat the pareve whipping cream until whipped; set aside.

In large bowl, combine the egg yolks, cocoa and vanilla. Fold the whipped topping into the chocolate mixture. Next, fold in the egg whites until well combined and cover. Place the bowl in the freezer and freeze until firm. This recipe can be doubled.

## Chocolate Mousse

This is a full-bodied, full-flavored clone of the cream-filled version. It can be dressed up or down, depending on the occasion; or even eaten out of the bowl, if you can't wait!

Makes 6 servings.

*¾ cup sugar*
*½ cup unsweetened cocoa*
*¼ cup water*
*1 tablespoon instant coffee granules*
*5 eggs, separated*
*½ teaspoon salt*
*2 tablespoons orange or almond liqueur*
*Almond slivers or pecan pieces for garnish*
*Non-dairy whipped topping for garnish*

In a saucepan, combine the sugar, cocoa, water and instant coffee. Cook over medium heat, stirring constantly until the mixture is smooth and thick, about 2–3 minutes; remove from the heat and cool slightly. In another mixing bowl, beat the egg yolks. Add the yolks to the chocolate mixture and cook for about 1 minute, stirring constantly; remove from the heat and cool.

In a separate mixing bowl, whip together the egg whites and salt until stiff. Stir the orange or almond liqueur into the chocolate mixture and mix well. Then, gently fold in the egg whites, ⅓ at a time.

Spoon the mousse into individual serving dishes or 1 large bowl. If desired, sprinkle with slivered almonds or pecan pieces, or garnish with a dollop of whipped non-dairy topping.

DAIRY OPTION: Beat ½–1 cup whipping cream together with 1–2 tablespoons powdered sugar; fold into the chocolate mixture just before adding the egg whites. Garnish the mousse with sweetened whipped cream.

## Pineapple Fluff

Kids love this stuff, but adults have been known to eat it, too.

Chill for 2 hours.
Makes 12 servings.

*2 eggs*
*⅔ cup sugar*
*4⅔ cups non-dairy creamer or rice milk*
*¼ cup plus 2 tablespoons instant tapioca*
*½ teaspoon salt*
*2 cups crushed pineapple, drained*
*16 large kosher marshmallows, quartered*
*2 cups frozen dessert topping*
*¼ cup chopped maraschino cherries*

In a mixing bowl, beat the eggs until light in color. Gradually beat in the sugar. Mix in the non-dairy creamer, tapioca and salt. Let stand 5 minutes. Transfer to a heavy saucepan and cook 4–5 minutes over medium-high heat, stirring frequently until the mixture comes to a boil; remove from the heat. Cover the pan with plastic wrap, pressing down on the pudding surface to prevent skin from forming. Let cool 20 minutes. Fold in the pineapple and marshmallows and chill. Fold in the whipped topping and cherries just before serving. Do not double this recipe.

# Chocolate Sorbet

This is the perfect antidote
to cure that chocolate craving.

Makes 6 servings.

*2½ cups water*
*¾ cup packed dark brown sugar*
*½ cup granulated sugar*
*⅔ cup unsweetened cocoa*
*Dash salt*
*2 tablespoons finely chopped bittersweet
chocolate*
*1½ teaspoons vanilla extract*
*1 teaspoon instant coffee*

Combine the water, brown sugar, granulated sugar, cocoa and salt in a saucepan. Bring to a boil over medium-high heat and cook, whisking occasionally, until the sugar dissolves, 4–5 minutes. Reduce the heat to low and boil gently for 3 minutes. Remove the syrup from the heat and add the chocolate, vanilla and coffee; whisk until the chocolate is melted and well mixed.

Pour the mixture into a bowl and place in the freezer until chilled but not frozen, stirring occasionally. When cold, transfer the mixture to an ice cream maker and process. Alternatively, let the mixture semi-freeze, then beat with a hand mixer; freeze until almost hard and beat with the hand mixer again. Let freeze hard and serve.

# Creamsicle Mousse

This is great with raspberries
or a raspberry or strawberry
coulis as a garnish.
Kids go crazy over this dessert.

Freeze at least 3 hours.
Makes 10–12 servings.

*2 cups non-dairy creamer*
*1 cup powdered orange drink, or 3
tablespoons frozen orange juice concentrate
plus 1 teaspoon orange extract*
*1½ cups non-dairy whipping cream*
*3 egg whites*
*¼ cup sugar*
*1 teaspoon vanilla*

In a bowl, combine the non-dairy creamer and orange drink powder or orange juice. Mix well. Pour half of the mixture into a 9x13-inch pan and freeze until firm. Refrigerate the remaining half of the mixture.

In a mixing bowl, beat the non-dairy whipping cream until semi-firm and set aside. In another bowl, beat the egg whites until they form stiff peaks; fold them into the whipped topping. Fold in the sugar and vanilla. Spread the whipped mixture over the frozen orange layer and freeze. When the "creamy" layer is firm, pour the remaining orange mixture over the top and return to the freezer. Freeze until firm. Cut into squares and serve.

133

# Blueberry Rhubarb Crisp with Pistachio Crust

It's tart and sweet and crunchy
all at the same time.

Bake at 375° for 50 minutes.
Serves 6–8.

### Filling:
⅓ cup granulated sugar
2 tablespoons all-purpose flour
2 cups rhubarb, cut into ½-inch pieces
2 cups (about 11 ounces) blueberries

### Topping:
⅓ cup pistachios
¾ cup all-purpose flour
½ cup granulated sugar
¼ cup packed brown sugar
¾ stick (6 tablespoons) cold margarine

Preheat oven. Grease a 2-quart shallow baking dish. In a bowl, stir together the sugar and flour. Add the rhubarb and bluberries and toss well. Spread the mixture in the prepared baking dish.

### Topping:

Finely chop the pistachios. In a bowl, whisk together the flour and sugars. Cut the margarine into ½-inch cubes and with a pastry blender or a fork blend the margarine into the flour mixture until the mixture resembles coarse meal. Add the pistachios and toss well. Squeeze a handful of the topping together and coarsely crumble in chunks over filling. Repeat until all the topping is evenly crumbled over the filling. Bake in upper third of oven until filling is bubbling and topping is crisp and golden. Serve warm or at room temperature.

# No-Bake Chocolate Balls

The perfect dessert for kids to make on a cold winter day or when it's too hot to play outside.

Let set for at least 30 minutes.
Makes about 20 balls.

1 cup margarine
¾ cup sugar
1½ cups quick oats
1½ cups shredded coconut
2 tablespoons cocoa
2 teaspoons rum, flavoring or real
4 teaspoons hot water
Coconut
Chocolate sprinkles

In a food processor, combine the margarine, sugar, oats, coconut and cocoa. Process until it's very fine. Add the rum and water and blend well. Shape ½ tablespoons into small balls and then roll them one by one either in shredded coconut or chocolate sprinkles. Let set. Keep cool, but not cold.

# Chocolate Overdose Cake

There is nothing like this cake. Anywhere, anytime, this is the answer to your craving for chocolate.

Bake at 325° for 45–60 minutes.
Makes 8–10 servings.

*1 cup cocoa*
*2 cups strong, hot coffee*
*3 cups all-purpose flour*
*2 teaspoons baking soda*
*½ teaspoon baking powder*
*Pinch of salt*
*4 eggs*
*1 cup softened margarine*
*2¼ cups sugar*
*2 teaspoons vanilla extract*
*½ teaspoon almond extract*
*6–8 diced maraschino cherries*
*¼ cup chocolate chips*

**Frosting:**
*2 cups whipped non-dairy topping*
*Chocolate syrup*

Preheat oven. Grease a 9x13-inch cake pan. In a small bowl, combine the cocoa and coffee, mixing until there are no lumps. In a separate, larger bowl, combine the dry ingredients and set them aside. In a third bowl, beat together the eggs, margarine, sugar, vanilla and almond extracts. Add ⅓ of the flour mixture to the egg mixture and then alternate adding the cocoa-coffee mixture and the flour mixture, finishing with the flour mixture. Gently fold in the cherries and chocolate chips before you add in the last of the flour mixture. Pour the batter into the prepared pan and bake, or until a toothpick inserted in center comes out clean (start checking at 45 minutes). This cake can get very dry if baked too long. Cool the cake completely and frost the top with the non-dairy topping. Drizzle the chocolate syrup over it in a decorative design.

# Rich Chocolate Cherry Cake

This is a very simple dessert
that's easy enough
for young children to make with
a minimum amount of supervision.

Bake at 350° for 1 hour.
Makes 8 servings.

2 cups all-purpose flour
¾ cup sugar
¾ cup vegetable oil
2 eggs
2 teaspoons vanilla
1 teaspoon baking soda
1 teaspoon cinnamon
21-ounce can cherry pie filling
⅓ cup semisweet chocolate chips
1 cup chopped walnuts
Confectioners' sugar for dusting

Preheat oven. In a large bowl, combine the flour, sugar, oil, eggs, vanilla, baking soda and cinnamon and mix well. Then stir in the pie filling, chocolate chips and nuts. Pour the batter into a greased bundt pan and bake. Cool 15–20 minutes; remove from the pan onto a cooling rack. Let cool at least 1 hour more. Dust with confectioners' sugar.

# Banana Split Cake

Better than its ice cream alternative
and a lot less messy!

Chill for 4 hours.
Makes 10–12 servings.

1½ cups graham cracker crumbs
1 cup softened margarine
2 cups powdered sugar
2 eggs
1½ cups crushed pineapple, drained well
3–4 ripe bananas
3 cups pareve whipped topping
1 cup cut up maraschino cherries
½ cup chopped pecans

In a large bowl, mix the graham cracker crumbs with ½ cup margarine. Press the mixture into a 13x9x2-inch oblong dish. Set aside. In a mixing bowl, combine the sugar, ½ cup margarine and eggs and beat until fluffy. Spread this mixture on top of the graham cracker crumbs. Pour the pineapple on top of the eggy layer. Slice the bananas and place them on top of the pineapple. Spread the whipped topping on top of the pineapple and sprinkle with the chopped pecans and maraschino cherries. Chill before serving. This can be made a day or two ahead, but needs to sit at room temperature for about 20 minutes before serving if it's been in the freezer more than 8 hours.

DAIRY OPTION: Substitute butter for the margarine and sweetened whipped cream for the whipped topping.

# Lemon Poppy Bundt Cake

A first-class cake that you can dress up with a fruit sauce or serve just as it is.

Bake at 350° for 35 minutes.
Makes 12 servings.

*1½ cups all-purpose flour*
*1½ cups cake flour, sifted*
*1½ cups sugar*
*2 teaspoons baking powder*
*1 teaspoon baking soda*
*¾ teaspoon salt*
*1½ cups unsweetened applesauce*
*3 tablespoons vegetable oil*
*3 tablespoons freshly squeezed lemon juice*
*1 tablespoon grated lemon rind*
*4 egg whites, at room temperature*
*¼ cup poppy seeds*

Preheat oven. Spray a 10-cup bundt pan with non-stick cooking spray; set aside. In a large bowl, whisk together the flours, 1 cup of sugar, baking powder, baking soda and salt. Set aside. In a medium-size bowl, whisk together the applesauce, oil, lemon juice and lemon rind until blended. In another medium-size bowl, using a mixer on high speed, beat the egg whites until foamy and almost double in volume. Slowly beat in the remaining ½ cup sugar until the whites form soft peaks. Make a well in the center of the flour mixture. Pour in the applesauce mixture and stir until just combined; the mixture will be quite thick. Stir about ¼ of the egg whites into the batter, then gently fold in the remaining egg whites; lastly, fold in the poppy seeds. Pour the batter into the prepared pan; shake gently to distribute the batter evenly. Bake until a toothpick inserted into the center comes out clean. Cool in its pan on a wire rack for 5 minutes; turn onto the rack to finish cooling. Do not double this recipe.

TIP: To keep a cake from falling when it is taken out of the oven, fill the pan with batter and before baking, lift it up and drop it suddenly on a table. This will release the air bubbles.

# Almond Raspberry Cake

This one is complicated
but is worth the extra effort.

Bake at 325° for 15–18 minutes.
Makes 12 servings.

### Cake:

¾ cup almond paste
½ cup sugar
¼ teaspoon salt
⅓ cup water
⅔ cup sifted cake flour
6 large egg whites
Pinch cream of tartar

### Filling and Meringue:

5 cups fresh or frozen raspberries
⅓ cup seedless raspberry preserves
3 large egg whites
½ cup sugar
¼ teaspoon cream of tartar
Confectioners' sugar for dusting

Preheat oven. Line the bottoms of two 9-inch round cake pans with parchment paper. Lightly coat the paper and pan sides with non-stick cooking spray, dust with flour, tapping out the excess and set aside.

In a food processor, combine the almond paste, ¼ cup of the sugar, salt and water; process until smooth. Add the flour and pulse until just combined. Transfer the mixture to a large bowl.

In a separate mixing bowl, beat the egg whites and cream of tartar with a mixer on high speed until frothy. While continuing to beat, slowly add the remaining ¼ cup sugar. Continue beating until soft peaks form. Whisk one-fourth of the beaten egg whites into the almond paste mixture. With a rubber spatula, fold in the remaining egg whites until just combined.

Spread the batter in the prepared pans. Bake until the cake layers are just beginning to color and feel firm when lightly pressed in the center. Dust a piece of parchment paper with confectioners' sugar. Run a knife around the outside edge of each cake layer to loosen and invert the cakes onto the paper. Remove the rounds of parchment paper from the cake bottoms. Let the cake layers cool to room temperature.

### Filling and meringue:

In a saucepan over medium heat, cook 3 cups of the raspberries, stirring constantly until the berries start to break up and become juicy. Strain through a sieve into a bowl. Press the fruit through and discard the seeds (do this twice if necessary). Return the purée to the saucepan. Cook over medium-low heat, stirring occasionally until thick and reduced to about ½ cup, about 5–10 minutes. Set aside ¼ cup of the purée.

Add the raspberry preserves to the purée remaining in the saucepan and whisk over low heat until smooth and slightly reduced, about 2 minutes; transfer to a large bowl to cool to room temperature.

Set aside about 30 of the best-looking raspberries to use as a garnish. Gently fold the rest of the raspberries into the cooled raspberry preserve mixture. With a wide spatula, invert one of the cake layers onto a heat-proof serving plate. Spread the raspberry mixture evenly over the top. Place the second cake layer on top. Set aside.

Combine the egg whites, sugar and cream of tartar in the top of a double boiler; set over simmering water and beat with an electric mixer on low speed, moving the beaters around the pot constantly, until an instant thermometer registers 140°. Increase the mixer speed to high and continue beating over the heat for a full 3½ minutes. Remove the top pot from the heat and beat the mixture until cooled to room temperature, about 5 minutes. On low speed, beat in the reserved ¼ cup of raspberry purée.

Preheat the broiler. Put about ⅔ cup of the meringue into a pastry bag fitted with a medium star tip. Spread the remaining meringue on the sides and top of the cake; smooth the sides and top with a long metal spatula. Pipe swirls of meringue around the edge of the cake using the pastry bag. With the cake about 2 inches below the heat source, broil until the top is lightly browned, about 1 minute. WATCH CAREFULLY.

Let cool, then decorate with the reserved raspberries. Just before serving, lightly dust the top with confectioners' sugar.

TIP: When making meringue shells, line the baking sheet with brown paper (from a bag) cut to fit.

TIP: To keep egg yolks, cover with cold water and store in the refrigerator for up to 3 days.

# French Lemon Cake

It's light and fresh and I promise there won't be any leftovers. This recipe should be made in a food processor.

Bake at 350° for 45 minutes.
Makes 12 servings.

*2 whole lemons*
*1 cup sugar*
*1 cup margarine*
*4 large eggs*
*3¾ cups all-purpose flour*
*2 teaspoons baking powder*
*1 cup powdered sugar*

Preheat oven. Peel the rind from the lemons. In a food processor or blender, process the sugar and lemon rind till the rind is finely chopped and well mixed. Add the margarine and blend well. Add eggs one by one and process. Add the flour and baking powder, process with a few quick on/off turns to just mix. Pour into a greased bundt pan and bake. Let set for 10 minutes; turn the cake out onto a rack and cool.

In a small bowl, squeeze the juice from the lemons and mix with the powdered sugar. Spoon the frosting slowly over the cake. You can add more powdered sugar to the frosting to make it thicker.

TIP: To make a fine-textured cake, add a few drops of boiling water to the shortening and sugar when creaming.

# Pistachio Harvest Cake

Bake at 350° for 1¼ hours.
Serves 12–14.

1½ cups vegetable oil
2 cups packed brown sugar
4 eggs
1 tablespoon vanilla extract
1 tablespoon lemon juice
½ tablespoon lemon zest
2 cups grated carrots
4 cups flour
1 tablespoon baking soda
4 teaspoons cinnamon
1 teaspoon nutmeg
1 teaspoon ginger
1 teaspoon salt
1 cup finely chopped pistachios
2 cups pareve sour cream
Orange Icing

Preheat oven. Mix the oil, sugar, eggs, vanilla, lemon juice, lemon zest and carrots in a large bowl. In a separate bowl, mix the flour, baking soda, cinnamon, nutmeg, ginger, salt and ¾ cup pistachios. Alternate adding the dry mixture and the pareve sour cream to the egg mixture, about a third at a time. Pour the batter into a greased and floured 14–cup bundt pan or crown ring mold. Bake until toothpick inserted into cake comes out dry. Cool 15 minutes in pan, then loosen top edges and gently invert from pan onto wire rack. When cake is completely cool, spread icing on top and decorate with remaining ¼ cup pistachios.

**Orange Icing:**

1 cup softened margarine
5 cups powdered sugar
1½ teaspoons grated orange peel
3–4 tablespoons orange juice

Beat the icing ingredients together with a mixer. Use just enough juice to make it a good, spreadable consistency.

NOTE: You can keep pistachios fresh by storing them in a refrigerated, airtight container, or keep them in the freezer. To restore their crispness, toast pistachios at 200° for 10–15 minutes. About ½ cup of pistachio nuts in the shell=¼ cup nutmeats.

# Macadamia Apricot Coffee Cake

You can make this fabulous
sweet and nutty treat in
less than a half-hour.

Bake at 375° for 18–25 minutes.
Serves 6–8.

*3½ ounces chopped macadamia nuts*
*¼ cup sugar*
*1 tablespoon flour*
*2 tablespoons softened margarine*
*1 egg, separated*
*1 sheet puff pastry dough*
*¼ cup apricot preserves*
*½ teaspoon grated orange peel*
*5 teaspoons sugar*
*1 tablespoon flour*
*2 teaspoons softened margarine*

**P**reheat oven. In a small bowl, combine ½ cup of the chopped macadamia nuts, ¼ cup sugar, 1
tablespoon flour, 2 tablespoons margarine and egg yolk; mix well. Set the
mixture aside.

Lay out the rectangular puff pastry
sheet and spread the prepared filling
lengthwise down the center ⅓ of the
rectangle. In a small bowl, combine
the preserves and orange peel. Spread
it over the filling.

To give a braided appearance to the
cake: On the outside thirds of the rectangle, make slices every inch and a
half from the top of the dough and
about 2½ inches in from the sides to
the bottom making sure not to cut too
close to the filling. Fold these "strips"
of dough at an angle across filling, alternating from side to side. Fold the
ends of the dough under to seal. Place
the coffee cake on an ungreased cookie
sheet. Beat the egg white slightly;
brush it over the top of the coffee
cake.

In a small bowl, combine the 5 teaspoons sugar, 1 tablespoon flour, 2
teaspoons margarine and remaining
macadamia nuts; mix until crumbly.
Sprinkle the crumbs evenly over the
top of the coffee cake. Bake until
golden. Warm 10–15 minutes before
serving.

## Extra-Moist Carrot Cake

This not-too-sweet cake works as a dessert or a side dish.

Bake at 350° for 45–60 minutes.
Makes 8–10 servings.

*1½ cups vegetable oil*
*2 cups sugar*
*4 eggs*
*2 cups all-purpose flour*
*2 teaspoons ground cinnamon*
*1½ teaspoons baking soda*
*½ teaspoon salt*
*3 cups grated carrots*
*1 orange, peel only*

In a large mixing bowl, beat together the oil and sugar. Add the eggs, one at a time, beating well after each addition. In another bowl, sift together the flour, cinnamon, baking soda and salt. Add to the egg mixture and beat well. Stir in the carrots and orange zest. Pour the batter into a greased 9x13-inch pan. Bake until a toothpick inserted in the center comes out clean.

DAIRY OPTION: When the cake cools, frost it with a cream cheese frosting.

## Upbeat Frosting

This recipe requires a lot of work, but makes a good impression.

Frosts 1 2-layer cake.

*2 eggs*
*1½ cups sugar*
*2 teaspoons light corn syrup*
*⅓ cup cold water*
*⅛ teaspoon salt*
*1½ teaspoons vanilla*

Place all of the ingredients, except the vanilla, in a double boiler and mix well. Beat continuously until the frosting begins to form peaks. Add the vanilla and continue beating until the frosting becomes spreadable. Do not double this recipe.

# Orange or Lemon Frosting

It's tangy and tart and terrific for a change-of-pace kind of frosting.

Makes about 2 cups or enough to frost 1 cake.

*½ cup shortening*
*3 cups powdered sugar*
*1 tablespoon grated orange or lemon zest*
*2–3 tablespoons orange or lemon juice*

Combine all the ingredients in a food processor or mixer and blend well. Add additional juice if necessary to make a spreadable consistency.

TIP: Lemons and limes won't turn brown if they are stored in water in the refrigerator.

# Super Frosting

Super doesn't begin to describe how great this frosting really is.

Makes about 4 cups or enough to frost a 2-layer cake.

*1 cup non-dairy creamer*
*¼ cup all-purpose flour*
*1 cup shortening*
*1 cup sugar*
*1 teaspoon vanilla*

In a saucepan, combine the non-dairy creamer with the flour and mix until smooth (a whisk works best). Cook over low heat, stirring constantly, until thick. Cool and set aside. With a mixer, cream together the shortening, sugar and vanilla. Beat in the cooled flour mixture and continue beating until fluffy and smooth.

OPTION: To make chocolate frosting, add 2 or more tablespoons cocoa powder to the hot liquid mixture before combining with the other ingredients.

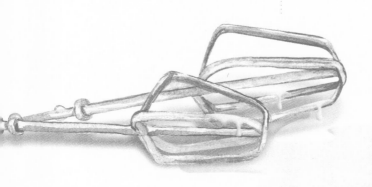

## Shiny Chocolate Frosting

An out-of-the-ordinary, fabulous frosting.

Frosts 1 cake.

*⅓ cup unsweetened chocolate*
*¼ cup margarine*
*3 cups powdered sugar*
*⅛ teaspoon salt*
*3–4 tablespoons heated non-dairy creamer*
*(or more, as needed)*
*1 teaspoon vanilla*

Place the chocolate and margarine in the top of a double boiler and heat until just melted. Pour the mixture into a mixing bowl and add the powdered sugar and salt. Add ⅓ of the non-dairy creamer, then the vanilla, and use a mixer to start beating. Continue beating and adding as much of the non-dairy creamer as needed until the mixture is spreadable.

MICROWAVE OPTION: To quickly prepare the chocolate and margarine, place them in a bowl and microwave until just melted. Then, proceed as above.

TIP: A sprinkling of flour or cornstarch on top of a cake will prevent the frosting from running off.

## E-Z Chocolate Frosting

This is easier than easy. Perfect for when you have helpers with more enthusiasm than skill.

Frosts 1 cake.

*3 tablespoons melted margarine*
*2 tablespoons cocoa*
*1½ cups powdered sugar*
*2 tablespoons non-dairy creamer or water*
*1 teaspoon vanilla*

Combine the margarine and cocoa in a large mixing bowl and mix well. Add the powdered sugar, non-dairy creamer (or water) and vanilla. Stir until smooth and then beat with a mixer until spreadable. This recipe can be doubled or tripled.

TIP: To quickly melt margarine, microwave in a microwave-safe bowl for 30–45 seconds on high power. Make sure to cover the bowl with plastic wrap, as the margarine may "bubble and pop."

# Coconut Nut Frosting

If you like coconut, you'll go nuts for this unique frosting.

Makes about 1 cup or enough to frost 1 cake.

*3 tablespoons melted margarine*
*5 tablespoons brown sugar*
*2 tablespoons non-dairy creamer*
*½ cup shredded coconut*
*½ cup chopped nuts*

Preheat broiler. In a large bowl, mix all the ingredients well. Spread the frosting on top of the cake while the frosting is still warm. Place the cake on the lowest oven rack and broil until the surface bubbles and becomes brown. Watch carefully so that it doesn't burn. This recipe can be doubled or tripled.

DAIRY OPTION: Substitute milk for non-dairy creamer and butter for shortening.

# Converting Measurements

## Weight Conversions

¼ pound = 4 ounces
½ pound = 8 ounces
¾ pound = 12 ounces
1 pound = 16 ounces

## Dry Measures

1 tablespoon = 3 teaspoons
¼ cup = 4 tablespoons
⅓ cup = 5 tablespoons + 1 teaspoon
½ cup = 8 tablespoons
1 cup = 16 tablespoons
1 pint = 2 cups
1 quart = 4 cups
1 pound = 16 ounces

## Liquid Measures

1 tablespoon = 3 teaspoons = ½ fluid ounce
1 fluid ounce = 2 tablespoons
¼ cup = 4 tablespoons = 2 fluid ounces
1 cup = 8 fluid ounces
1 pint = 2 cups = 16 fluid ounces
1 quart = 2 pints = 4 cups
1 gallon = 8 pints = 4 quarts = 16 cups

## Linear Measures

0.394 inch = 1 centimeter
1 inch = 2.54 centimeters
39.37 inches = 1 meter

## Conversion Tables for Metric Equivalents

The exact value of each conversion appears in bold at the head of each list.
To facilitate quick referencing, all other values have been rounded off.

### OUNCES, POUNDS, GRAMS, KILOS

**1 ounce = 28.35 grams**
**1 pound = 454 grams**
**2.2 pounds = 1000 grams = 1 kilogram**

| | |
|---|---|
| 1 oz. = 30 gr. | 2 lb. = 910 gr. |
| 2 oz. = 60 gr. | 2¼ lb. = 1025 gr. = 1 kg. |
| 3 oz. = 85 gr. | 2½ lb. = 1140 gr. |
| ¼ lb. = 4 oz. = 115 gr. | 2¾ lb. = 1250 gr. |
| 5 oz. = 140 gr. | 3 lb. = 1365 gr. |
| 6 oz. = 170 gr. | 3½ lb. = 1590 gr. = 1½ kg. |
| 7 oz. = 200 gr. | 4 lb. = 1820 gr. |
| ½ lb. = 8 oz. = 225 gr. | 4½ lb. = 2045 gr. = 2 kg. |
| 9 oz. = 255 gr. | 5 lb. = 2270 gr. |
| 10 oz. = 285 gr. | 5½ lb. = 2500 gr. = 2½ kg. |
| 11 oz. = 310 gr. | 6 lb. = 2730 gr. |
| ¾ lb. = 12 oz. = 340 gr. | 6½ lb. = 2955 gr. = 3 kg. |
| 13 oz. = 370 gr. | 7 lb. = 3180 gr. |
| 14 oz. = 395 gr. | 8 lb. = 3640 gr. = 3½ kg. |
| 15 oz. = 425 gr. | 9 lb. = 4090 gr. = 4 kg. |
| 1 lb. = 16 oz. = 455 gr. | 10 lb. = 4540 gr. = 4½ kg. |
| 17 oz. = 485 gr. | 11 lb. = 4995 gr. = 5 kg. |
| 18 oz. = 510 gr. | |
| 1¼ lb. = 20 oz. = 570 gr. | |
| 22 oz. = 625 gr. | |
| 1½ lb. = 24 oz. = 680 gr. | |
| 26 oz. = 740 gr. | |
| 1¾ lb. = 28 oz. = 795 gr. | |
| 30 oz. = 850 gr. | |
| 2 lb. = 32 oz. = 910 gr. | |

## CUPS, FLUID OUNCES, LITERS

*1 ounce = 29.56 milliliters*
*33.83 ounces = 1 liter*

1 oz. = 30 ml.
¼ cup = 2 oz. = 60 ml.
3 oz. = 90 ml.
½ cup = 4 oz. = 120 ml.
5 oz. = 150 ml.
6 oz. = 175 ml.
7 oz. = 205 ml.
1 cup = 8 oz. = 235 ml.
9 oz. = 265 ml.
10 oz. = 295 ml.
1½ cups = 12 oz. = 355 ml.
14 oz. = 415 ml.
2 cups = 16 oz. = 475 ml.
18 oz. = 530 ml.
2½ cups = 20 oz. = 590 ml.
22 oz. = 650 ml.
3 cups = 24 oz. = 710 ml.
26 oz. = 770 ml.
3½ cups = 28 oz. = 830 ml.
30 oz. = 885 ml.
4 cups = 32 oz. = 945 ml.
4½ cups = 36 oz. = 1.1 liters
5 cups = 40 oz. = 1.2 liters
8 cups = 64 oz. = 1.9 liters
16 cups = 128 oz. = 3.8 liters

## TEMPERATURE EQUIVALENTS

*°Farenheit = (°C x 9/5) + 32*
*°Centigrade = (°F − 32) x 5/9*

32 °F = 0 °C
60 °F = 16 °C
80 °F = 27 °C
100 °F = 38 °C
125 °F = 52 °C
140 °F = 60 °C
150 °F = 66 °C
160 °F = 71 °C
175 °F = 80 °C
180 °F = 82 °C
190 °F = 88 °C
200 °F = 95 °C
212 °F = 100 °C
225 °F = 107 °C
250 °F = 120 °C
275 °F = 135 °C
300 °F = 150 °C
325 °F = 165 °C
350 °F = 175 °C
375 °F = 190 °C
400 °F = 205 °C
425 °F = 220 °C
450 °F = 230 °C
475 °F = 245 °C
500 °F = 260 °C
525 °F = 275 °C
550 °F = 290 °C

# *Index*

If you are looking for an appetizer or salad to make, simply turn to the appropriate section opening page and you will see a list of all the recipes, including their page numbers, that are found in that section. If, however, you have an ingredient in your kitchen that you would like to use up (such as bananas or potatoes), you can consult this index, under the ingredient's name. This index also lists every recipe in alphabetical order. I hope I've made your search both easy and practical.

*Notes*